1,00

# Is This Really What I Want To Do?

## PREVIOUS BOOKS BY THE AUTHOR

*Be The Person You Were Meant To Be*
*Creative Intimacy*

# Is This Really What I Want To Do

## Dr. Jerry Greenwald

**Ward Ritchie Press**
Pasadena, California

I wish to thank Charleen Williams
and Mary Tibbles for their diligent
efforts in the preparation of this
manuscript.

**To Fritz Perls and Jim Simkin**

*with deep appreciation for helping me become more aware of what I really want to do.*

# Preface

*Throughout our lives there is an ongoing question we may ask ourselves at any time: "Is this how I want to use up this hour, this evening, or this day of my life?" Or—"Is there something more gratifying, more nourishing, more creative I would rather be doing?"*

There is a simplicity about life, which is infinitely rich and meaningful. We complicate our lives with a wilderness of trivia, distorted goals, and tension-producing attitudes and beliefs. We lose contact with the essential nourishing aspects of life as we continue to create a social environment already so complex that it threatens to overwhelm us. We are constantly in danger of being misled, deceived and manipulated by others who, either with sincere conviction in the rightness of their purposes or for their own selfish ends, seek to control us.

The question "Is this really what I want to do?" can make us aware of the need to maintain personal freedom in the face of these external influences. Asking it does not imply that we are impulsive, defiant or rebellious, or that we in any way ignore the realistic consequences of our behavior. Rather, it suggests that we privately adopt, and resolve to live by, a personal commitment to regulate our own lives.

When we ask ourselves "What do I really want right now?" we may feel lost, confused or in conflict, because learning to trust our natural responses to life brings us face to face with powerful opposition, the opposition of our toxic myths.

Each of us, particularly during childhood, has been indoctrinated with attitudes, beliefs and values we have never thought to question or to fit to our concepts of ourselves. Obsolete or false attitudes, beliefs and values that violate our realities or restrict us unnecessarily are toxic to us. They are our toxic myths. We are their victims. And the more we are victimized, the less loving, the less caring, the less joyful, the less wholesome we become in relating to ourselves and others. When we discover how to diminish the power of these poisonous patterns, our natural, healthy selves emerge. We can decide for ourselves whether we need to continue complicating our existences by complying with these myths, or whether we can discard them without detrimental effects to ourselves, our relationships with others, or our society.

A man was imprisoned in a dungeon. His only light came through one tiny crevice for a short time each day when the sun was at its peak. Even his food and water were passed to him in utter darkness. Each day the man would look forward to this brief period of time during which he would press close to the crevice so that he might catch a glimpse of some tiny part of the outside world. Then he would resign himself to total darkness until the next day. At first the man tried to explore his surroundings by feeling along the walls of the dungeon. When he discovered he was imprisoned in a cavernous area, he became afraid that, if he wandered too far, he would not be able to find his way back to the spot where this precious ray of light shone through each day. He never discovered that at the far end of the dungeon was an unlocked door leading to freedom.

In the same way, toxic myths create a fantasy prison in which we hold ourselves captive because we fear to explore or question. Unaware of our ability (or too intimidated) to explore the many ways in which we keep ourselves imprisoned, we cling to obsolete and unrealistic attitudes and behavior which we believe we *must* perpetuate because we have been told we must or should, or because we believe everyone else does.

This book examines some of these toxic myths. It shows how most of us cling to them and, in the process, dissipate our life energies and diminish our well-being and our capacity for growth. It also explores antidotes to these obsolete attitudes and beliefs and suggests approaches that might free our energies for more meaningful and gratifying endeavors.

This, then, is a book about freedom, the freedom to live our lives as we choose in a society in which external powers of many kinds seek to regulate more and more of our existence. These external powers increasingly intrude into that area of living we call our intimate personal existence. Regardless of our status or chosen role in life, each of us is affected by these pressures, for almost everyone would like to tell us how we *should* be, what we *should* believe in, what we *should* stand for, what we *should* stand against, and how we *should* live our lives.

In this book, as in my previous books, I have utilized the philosophy of Gestalt with its attendant validation of a quest for naturalness. My intent is to help all of us clear away the artificial complexities with which we repress our aliveness. The more effective we are in doing this, the more we discover that simplicity in living is synonymous with naturalness, joy and creativity. But toxic myths often hamper our quest. They make more difficult our struggle to live as we really choose to, without guilt, shame or fear of social consequences. By asking "Is this really what I want to do?" we exercise our freedom to seek and discover our changing selves and to create personal existences in which decisions regarding our social behavior are based on preserving this inner freedom and assuming responsibility for it.

# Contents

**Nourishing and Toxic Myths    1**

**Is This Really What I Want To Do
With My Personal Life?    10**

Guilt, Shame and Fear    11
Selfishness Myths    17
The Taboo Against Tears    20
The Taboo Against Conflicts    23
The Taboo Against Mistakes    31

**Is This Really What I Want To Do
With My Family Life?    34**

Myths About the Family    35
Myths About Parents and
    Parenthood    39
Myths About Marriage    42
Thou Shalt Answer All Questions    51
Childhood: The Helpless Victim    54

**Is This Really What I Want To Do
With My Life In Society?    70**

Myths About Human Behavior    71
The Punishment Myth    75
Myths About Living    79
What's In A Name?    83

Sacred Cows: Myths about
  Heroes and Experts   89
Myths About the Medical World   92
Myths About Death and Dying   96


**Is This Really What I Want To Do
With My Working Life?   100**

The Myth of Normalcy   101
The Popularity Contest   107
Performance Myths   113
Myths About Work and Play   131


**Is This Really What I Want To Do
With My Sex Life?   140**

Myths About Sex   141
Victorian Mythology   151
More Is Better   163
Was I Good?   164
What Do You Like?   166


**Nourishing and Toxic Societies   171**

**How To Recognize Toxic Myths   183**

**Antidotes To Toxic Myths   195**

# Is This Really What I Want To Do?

# Nourishing and Toxic Myths

A myth as defined here is a popular idea that is either an out-and-out lie or a gross distortion of reality and reflects attitudes and beliefs that have been traditionally accepted as valid. These attitudes and beliefs have been nurtured, protected and perpetuated for generations and continue to be accepted as appropriate without current question or examination. This book focuses on myths about human nature: what a human being *should* be like, or what kind of behavior *should* normally be expected.

Each myth has accompanying taboos and rituals that have evolved from it. The myth itself expresses an attitude or belief, and its taboos and rituals are the behavior patterns that are encouraged (rituals) or prohibited (taboos) to ensure compliance with the myth.

## Nourishing Myths

Myths are part of the world of fantasy concocted by human beings and handed down from generation to generation. When they are accepted as the fairy tales they are, they may enrich a culture and enhance the individual's sense of belonging.

Nourishing myths do not violate the freedom to experience ourselves and our world in our own way. Nor do they instill fear, guilt and shame when we choose to reject them. Nourishing myths include much of the folklore of a culture, stories and fables about its historical past that contribute to its identity and uniqueness. They are part of the social heritage that provides members of each new generation with a sense of belonging to something larger than their separate selves. In this sense, a nourishing mythology is an inherited part of the societal security system, a source of strength that encourages the growth and enhances the well-being of its individual members.

We can best understand the difference between nourishing and toxic myths by considering the effect of a particular myth on us as individuals, as well as on our society as a whole. Nourishing myths foster exhilaration, excitement and positive attitudes toward ourselves, others and the world in which we live. They encourage feelings of contentment, joy and creativity. Nourishing myths encourage these attitudes toward ourselves and others without creating antagonists (scapegoats). They do not alienate us from others. They do not make "enemies" of others who have different characteristics, attitudes or beliefs. Similarly, nourishing myths are not antagonistic toward any group of human beings anywhere on earth.

**One of the hallmarks of toxic myths is that they create antagonists and then build a set of attitudes and beliefs dedicated to protection from, or destruction of, the enemy they have created.**

Nourishing myths are those we choose to believe in because they add value, meaning *and* richness to our lives without intruding on the well-being of others. Nourishing myths enhance our appreciation of being human. They whet our appetite for the possibilities of discovering more about ourselves and our world.

## Toxic Myths

Myths are toxic when they impose unnecessary restrictions on individual freedom. Some source of authority continuously enforces these myths and resists change in the face of changing reality. The evolution of social change takes generations. During this time various kinds of authorities often use their power to induce guilt, shame and fear (as opposed to reason, common sense and realistic necessity) to perpetuate traditional myths, taboos and rituals regardless of how obsolete and poisonous they have become.

The history of a particular toxic myth usually reveals that at one time it served some need of the group but gradually became nonadaptive and toxic. For example, we can describe the sequence in which a nourishing myth becomes toxic by considering a primitive society in which hunting is the primary source of food:

1. The group discovers that, while hunting dangerous animals, some men become frightened and run away. Their actions threaten the group's food supply and render the remaining hunters more vulnerable to attack.

2. The group develops rules and regulations that punish a hunter who abandons the hunting party.

3. Fear becomes increasingly taboo while bravery earns the approval of the group. Social approval is gradually formalized through rituals and ceremonies honoring those whose exploits demonstrate outstanding bravery. They become heroes. The system works. The group's ability to

feed itself is enhanced, and the safety of the individual hunter is more assured. The rules are preserved and taught to each new generation.

4. Through succeeding generations a folklore develops that includes mythical tales of bravery and cowardice by hunters of past generations. With time these myths become distorted or exaggerated to enhance the values the group wants to emphasize. Heroes of uncanny bravery become the envy of every child, while the taboo against cowardice becomes deeply rooted.

5. At some point in time, game diminishes as an adequate source of food, and the group, of necessity (changing reality), increasingly turns to farming for its food. By now the taboos against fear have been so deeply entrenched that fearfulness under any circumstances or conditions is held in contempt.

6. Despite the major change in their life-style, the rituals developed in an earlier era of the group culture continue to be enforced. As part of the group's puberty rites, each boy must kill a large and dangerous animal single-handledly to demonstrate his bravery and ability as a hunter. Those who pass the rites are accepted as first-class citizens and are allowed to choose wives. Those who fail are ostracized and may not marry. Each year, a number of males are killed or injured in the performance of this ritual. In addition, those males who excel as farmers and supply the food in this agrarian society not only go unrewarded but are deprived of their right to a wife if they fail during the traditional puberty rites. The myths about fearlessness and bravery and the taboos and rituals that follow from them have now become toxic; however, the toxic myth that physical prowess and bravery are higher values than whatever qualities make a man or woman a productive farmer has been so formalized that it persists, in spite of its obsolescence. It is perpetuated by each new generation of

those who pass the hunting rituals and benefit personally from doing so.

**Toxic Myth: A real man is fearless.**

**Toxic Myth: Women are inferior to men because they are physically weaker and less effective hunters.**

In the above example, it made sense in a tribe of hunters that each male be tested for his strength and bravery when his own life, the lives of his fellow hunters, and the survival of the group depended on his skills and courage. As the society developed in complexity and required a diversity of roles, the need for individual physical prowess and courage in the face of danger became less critical, while other kinds of individual abilities became increasingly valuable. Toxic myths ignore such social changes and persist in demanding universal conformity to less important, often obsolete values. The gunfighter of the Old West is still considered in our contemporary myths as more masculine than the farmer; the war hero, more manly than the research scientist.

Other toxic myths dampen our enthusiasm for life. They hinder the potential we have for meaningful experiences and growth. Some ominously warn us, explicitly or implicitly, that we have "instincts" that by their very existence threaten destruction to ourselves or others and must be guarded like savage animals locked in cages.

All such toxic myths, with their repressive demands, are manipulative. Most are outright lies. They are arbitrarily enforced and not subject to compromise, reason or examination. Those dedicated to their perpetuation relentlessly strive to instill their repressive, restrictive attitudes in all of us, not just those who choose to believe them.

Every culture has attitudes and beliefs accepted for generations and which, in various ways, distort human reality. These are toxic to the degree that they foster unrealistic social expectations about how we *should* think, feel and behave, how we *should* react, and what attitudes we *should* *have toward ourselves and others.*

Toxic myths about the need to control our personal behavior in the way we relate to others teach us that we are basically untrustworthy, unreliable — even unpredictable.

When our attitudes and behavior do not comply with mythical expectations, we are made to feel that something is wrong or we would not fail to react properly and meet the goals these myths demand. Toxic myths also lead us to believe that everyone else (except for a few rebels and misfits) is comfortable in accepting these social expectations. The overall effect is a vicious cycle of increasing feelings of alienation and inadequacy about ourselves.

Toxic myths share a common attitude that individual uniqueness is undesirable, wrong or even evil. They hinder the quest for our own unique identity by denying our right to a personal, private existence based on our chosen values and the particular life-style that suits us best. This restrictive process is often administered with an attitude of indifference. The individual is not committing any crime nor is he or she encroaching on the rights of others. He or she is simply guilty of not fitting in and conforming to the social expectations a particular myth requires.

Many so-called neurotic patterns (and some are labeled

psychotic) are nothing more than the reflections of these arbitrary attitudes and beliefs that comprise the toxic mythology of our society. When these violate natural human behavior too drastically and compliance is too rigidly enforced, toxic myths, rituals and taboos become a powerful social pressure causing unnecessary emotional tensions and psychological stress and can lead to serious mental and physical problems in some of their victims. There is no doubt, for example, that irrational guilt based on toxic myths has driven many people insane.

The authority structure that implements this social pressure is, of course, composed of other members of society, most of whom we can assume are sincere in their belief that the taboos and rituals they insist on enforcing are necessary. They consider themselves to be socially minded and are frequently dedicated individuals interested in the common good of the whole group.

What makes their role toxic is the quality of self-righteousness with which they go about the business of enforcing their beliefs on everyone. They function with a close-minded attitude typical of dogmatic, authoritarian personalities. They are unwilling, even unable, to be open-minded enough to consider viewpoints other than their own. Because violators are automatically considered as guilty, the only issues they are concerned with are punishment and ultimate conformity by everyone.

Closer examination reveals that, coupled with their attitude of virtue and self-righteousness, is a sense of personal gratification. They enjoy the power they have over others. Some are able to maintain or achieve economic and social advantages. Others use this role as a way of avoiding the insecurities and anxieties that accompany social change or a lack of uniform adherence to the status quo. For them, change of any kind poses a threat to their inner well-being.

**One of the hallmarks of a toxic myth is that some segment of society benefits from its perpetuation, and the accompanying taboos and rituals, to the detriment of others.**

This segment of society always has some power to punish. In our culture, those who violate the taboos and rituals are made to feel guilty, shameful or fearful.

Nourishing myths are *not* enforced by any authority within the culture. The Santa Claus myth is part of the nourishing mythology of our culture. There is little demand on us that we believe in Santa Claus. Some choose to enjoy this myth especially with young children and feel that it adds richness to their lives. Others ignore the Santa Claus myth and are free to do so without fear of punishment or reprisal.

**Another hallmark of toxic myths is their intolerance of dissent.**

Unchallengeability is a built-in aspect of toxic myths. Challenging a myth violates the taboo intrinsic to all toxic mythology: the taboo against questioning. Toxic myths, with their mutually reinforcing constellation of taboos and rituals, cripple our ability to evolve the personal sense of identity we can best discover in a social atmosphere in which experimentation is acceptable. As children, we must submit to well-meaning parents and teachers or be filled with guilt and shame. Usually, it is only when we approach adulthood that we have the freedom and personal power to experiment and evolve our own attitudes, values and beliefs. Even then, toxic myths, with their accompanying taboos and rituals, are not negotiable. There is always the risk of social pressure when we take a stand against blind conformity to them.

The major portion of all human guilt is irrational and is based solely on having been indoctrinated into believing that various feelings, thoughts or impulses within us simply wouldn't be there if we were the right kind of person, and that thinking of a taboo thought or impulse is the same as acting on it.

A toxic myth persists only so long as it is continuously and forcefully perpetuated by a source of authority to which we have surrendered some of our personal power. Otherwise it would gradually lose its power. We assist in perpetuating toxic myths when we accept them automatically and ignore our awareness of their ill effects. Unknowingly, many of us have lost our senses. We fail to distinguish ideas, values and behavior that are nourishing and meaningful from others that are toxic and meaningless.

# Is This Really What I Want To Do With

# My Personal Life

## Guilt, Shame and Fear

As we begin to focus more specifically on the most pervasive toxic myths in our culture, one in particular stands out as the most powerful and the most destructive of all: _the guilt myth_. Once we are sufficiently indoctrinated with this fundamental myth, we are helpless against the manipulations of the adult world. This myth undermines our intuitive ability to distinguish that which is wholesome and healthy in relationships and that which is not. All that we need to learn can be taught with love and without using guilt, shame and fear.

**TOXIC MYTH #1**
**We must feel guilty, for unless guilt restrains us, we will run amuck.**

Our poisoning with this toxic myth begins in early childhood. Deeply ingrained guilt myths teach us that human beings are essentially evil and naturally destructive: a fear of punishment for our trangressions is the only basis on which a society can survive. This myth becomes a self-fulfilling prophecy when it instills in us deep feelings of distrust toward ourselves and others. Many people live their entire lives fearing that, were they to allow themselves to act out all their emotions and impulses, they would lose control and something disastrous would surely follow. They frighten themselves with this myth particularly when they feel very intense emotions. When, for example, their anger does well up, despite their efforts to suppress it, they become frightened of going berserk, perhaps even killing someone. (After all, such crimes do happen!) this myth would have us live our lives as if we were all constantly in danger of committing murder. In reality, the taboo against expressing anger is much more likely to generate the emotional explosiveness that results in a loss of control and real violence.

The guilt myth teaches us to feel the same pain for a socially unacceptable impulse that we might expect to experience if we had actually transgressed against someone or committed some criminal act. In its extreme form, it creates an all-encompassing blanket of taboos against everything we think, feel or do that might generate any feeling of guilt. It teaches us to equate feeling guilty with being wrong. It easily lends itself to being used by adults to manipulate children by "putting the fear in them."

The most popular toxic technique used by parents to control their children is inducing guilt by condemning natural feelings and attitudes. The child who will not share his or her candy is made to feel guilty for being "selfish," which is also taboo in our society. In adulthood, submission to irrational guilt continues when we impose demands on ourselves or allow others to impose demands on us largely out of fear that we will feel guilty if we refuse to comply.

The most direct antidote to the poison of guilt-induced myths is allowing ourselves to be in touch with but not necessarily act out, all our inner thoughts, feelings and impulses. This is the most natural way for each of us to learn what feelings and impulses we want to express or restrain. Toxic myths about "evil" thoughts and feelings —that is, thoughts that make us feel guilty—are a stacked deck against us because we imagine we are wrong or even crazy to have them in the first place. When we take responsibility for governing ourselves and our actions, we are less likely to give over this freedom to someone else.

**TOXIC MYTH #2**
**Feeling guilt means we must have done something wrong.**

To live dominated by the guilt myth is a way of never becoming oneself and never feeling trustworthy. Victims of the myth often live with endless fears and fantasies of retribution from the external world—all based on irrational guilt. Those who live in fear of violating the taboo against feeling guilty are themselves the main perpetuators of the guilt myth because they, in turn, manipulate others (for example, their children) with similar guilt tactics when they have the opportunity.

Another ritual of the guilt myth demands that we must somehow "cleanse" ourselves of our guilt feelings before we can be free to live our own lives. Because we are dealing with an irrational process in the first place, this struggle is endless and futile. (The irrational guilt discussed here is different from that based on religious beliefs or religious dogma. Guilt based on the violations of religious teachings takes on different considerations. Irrational guilt, in contrast, is strictly man-made. Chronic victims of the guilt myth are usually convinced that they are permanently disqualified as fully acceptable human beings.

**TOXIC MYTH #3**
**A feeling of shame means we are a failure.**

Guilt has a twin poisoner: *shame.* Shame is a feeling (or fear) of failure as a human being. The victims of irrational guilt are almost invariably also ashamed of themselves. They are self-condemning human beings who see themselves as personal and social failures despite how others might view them. Like the victims of the guilt myth, those who fall prey to shame myths develop a false (and impossible) image of what they must do to be exonerated. Typically, they create an idealized image of themselves that either demands perfection, or at least insists that they *must* and *should* improve constantly.

Each of us has an idealized image consisting of all the ways toxic myths teach us we must be to avoid feeling ashamed. Trying to conform to this image is like living in an emotional straitjacket. All idealized images are devastating because of their insatiable demands that we strive to become something more or better than we are. Perfection is not a human quality. The quest for it is a disease fostered to avoid inner feelings of shame. In reality, each person's idealized image is his or her own self-induced curse.

> **The antidote to the taboos against shame and guilt is to allow ourselves to feel ashamed or guilty and, in spite of these feelings, do what we want to do or are willing to do (or not to do) for ourselves and others.**

Guilt and shame, like fear and anxiety, are part of every person's emotional experience. When we use them to avoid being the kind of person we want to be, they become nothing more than excuses, however painful, for not taking responsibility for our own existence. A nourishing attitude toward ourselves, when we wish to live our own lives, requires no prior qualifying or proving. These are nothing but rituals demanded by the guilt and shame myths. When we are unwilling to live our lives as we choose, we will wait forever for others to tell us we are entitled to do so. And even should that great day come, we won't believe them because irrational guilt and shame do not respond to rational achievements, virtue or exoneration from others.

**TOXIC MYTH #4**
**Fear is a weakness, something we should**
**try to overcome.**

Fear is a natural response to threat, danger or the unknown, yet we are taught that we should never be afraid.
While countless expectations are placed on us that threat-
en disapproval or rejection should we fail to perform
properly, we are told not to be afraid of failure, not to be
afraid of disapproval, not to be afraid of those with the
power to punish us. Parents are portrayed as loving and
caring on the one hand, while their actions toward their
children foster feelings of guilt, shame, and fear of punishment, actual or threatened. Yet it is taboo for the child to
be afraid of those who love him.

The taboo against fear constricts our aliveness in many
ways. We learn to avoid or conceal those thoughts, feelings and actions that might reveal our fearfulness. The
taboo against fear inhibits our natural eagerness to experiment with life, restricts our potential growth and hampers
our ability to discover greater fulfillment and meaning in
our lives.

**Like guilt and shame, fear is an automatic**
**no-no that, in turn, enhances another**
**taboo: the taboo against experimenting**
**with life.**

The guilt, shame and fear myths create a triangular prison
trapping us in lives of ritualistic conformity to taboos
against thinking, feeling or doing anything that is not
clearly sanctioned by society. They tend to make children
into robots programmed by the toxic mythology of our
culture. We learn to respond in a ritualistic manner that

keeps us safely within the bounds of group conformity. We become paper people responding with platitudes, clichés and vague generalities. We gradually, and usually without awareness, bury our real feelings beneath "normal" responses, those the group sanctions. Eventually we feel only what we *should* feel.

There is no end to this struggle to avoid the fear of tabooed thoughts, feelings and actions. In the quest to feel secure, more and more of our selves is lost as we listen to the dictates of our social computer. We become deaf, dumb and blind to internal or external stimuli that might encourage feelings, thoughts or actions that do not fit into this social program. When such impulses do emerge, as they invariably do, more toxic manipulations of the self become necessary. For example, many people are frightened by their own sexual feelings. They learn to project this "evil" away from themselves and onto the "irresponsible" mass media. They insist that, without the sexual stimulation of films and literature, they would not feel lust or want to act out their sexual impulses.

In every such instance, the inner reality of what we are really like as individuals is distorted to maintain a self-image that does not violate the toxic myths, taboos and rituals of our society. Thus we lose ourselves in an endless struggle to avoid guilt, shame and fear.

Ironically, despite all our efforts to suppress them, our natural feelings and impulses constantly seek expression and thus we become trapped in a continuous process of trying to repress natural impulses. The poisonous effects on us are twofold. First, despite our best efforts to avoid confronting ourselves with such unacceptable impulses, our defensive maneuvers are never entirely effective. Socially unacceptable thoughts, feelings and impulses do expose themselves in subtle ways. Thus we develop a concept of ourselves as inadequate and deficient in some of the more desirable human qualities. Or, even more devastating, we develop a basic lack of self-worth and self-trust and a growing belief that we are intrinsically bad or evil individuals. Second, in the struggle to maintain a socially acceptable image of ourselves, we constantly use energy to suppress threatening thoughts, feelings and impulses. Thus spent, this energy is lost to us and cannot be put to more constructive, creative or meaningful uses in experiencing life. Struggling with our guilt, shame and fear renders us unable to live fully.

## Selfishness Myths

Selfishness myths are probably the most common and the most widespread of all those toxic myths that would have us believe our natural, spontaneous behavior must be stifled. Most of us have been raised to believe that "selfishness' is a dirty word. By implication, any manifestation of selfishness must be suppressed; otherwise, it could emerge with such overwhelming power that it would dominate our entire behavior. This idea that the impulses we release by expression will overwhelm us is a prime example of the Pandora's Box attitude inherent in toxic myths. We must keep the lid on at all costs.

The irony of this lie is that the most effective control over our impulses involves learning to express them frequently, in moderation and without feeling guilty. When we give reasonable expression to an impulse, we become satisfied and the power of that impulse is diminished. In contrast, when we refuse to allow the expression of a particular impulse, it grows stronger and harder to subdue, and we become more frightened of it. Toxic myths encourage us to develop this "tight little box" attitude toward our impulses. By unnatural and unhealthy suppression, we actually increase the possibility that a repressed impulse will explode in socially unacceptable behavior.

Selfishness is a manifestation of self-preservation, an instinct found in all living creatures. Yet is it taboo for us to acknowledge openly the obvious: that each of us is the most important person in the world to ourselves. Each of us must take responsibility for ourselves and our well-being if we are to survive. It is not possible for someone else to do this for us even if he or she would want to.

**TOXIC MYTH #5**
**When we put our own needs ahead of others' needs, we are inconsiderate, uncaring individuals.**

Selfishness (self-ness) does not adversely affect our ability to love others or our willingness to give and do for them. If anything, selfishness, our purposeful efforts to satisfy our own needs and provide for our own well-being, is the most natural way of becoming more truly giving *and* more capable of responding to other's needs.

The taboo against selfishness implies that we gratify our needs *at the expense of someone else,* that when we sustain our own well-being, we are depriving others. This toxic attitude only enhances feelings of guilt and resentment. It does not make us less selfish or more giving. Rather, our natural givingness is transformed into an unnatural kind of "giving" to avoid feeling guilty or to exonerate ourselves from existing guilt feelings.

Children are told that they are bad when they put their own needs first or feel possessive about their personal possessions and refuse to share. Sharing becomes a ritualistic demand that we act unselfish toward others or bear the pain of guilt and shame. Children learn that giving feels "good" because it brings relief from unpleasant, even unbearable guilt feelings.

When parents accuse their children of being selfish, their accusations often reflect their own selfishness. Parents' needs are often in conflict with those of their children. Parental demands that, for example, big sister read to little brother are often the parent's way of concealing his or her own unwillingness to perform the task. When big sister refuses because she wants to listen to her stereo, she is called selfish. The joy of her own activity is lessened as she is made to feel guilty because of her unwillingness to meet the equally selfish needs of her parents. In innumerable such circumstances, the taboo against selfishness takes its steady toll in our struggle to build the self-love and self-esteem essential for real givingness.

---

**TOXIC MYTH #6**
**Wanting to be the center of attention is wrong.**

---

*How come you always want to be the center of attention?* This question usually elicits feelings of shame, embarrassment or guilt. A myth is a corrupt teacher. Selfishness myths teach us to frown on all kinds of self-centeredness. Most of us grow up feeling that there is something bad about wanting attention—especially a lot of it! To admit freely that we enjoy being the center of attention is taboo. During childhood, most of us are encouraged to be quiet or "behave" (so that adults can be the center of attention).

When we are reasonably aware of our needs, each of us can list ways, including various manipulations of others, in which we gain the spotlight. Everyone wants to be the center of attention at times. Because this desire is taboo, we must gain attention through various socially accepted rituals. When an athlete wins a contest, it is socially acceptable to be the center of attention, provided he or she exhibits a certain ritual modesty. It is taboo to admit frankly that one deserves the acclaim of the crowd. Doing so brands the offender as a poor sport and causes us to hope that someone will quickly humble the person.

The Western movie usually conforms to the modesty ritual. The bad guy, an utterly obnoxious, boastful braggart, dominates each scene, insisting on his right to be the center of attention. The hero, in contrast, is typically quiet, modest and unassuming. In part, it is the taboo against wanting attention that arouses our resentment so that we back the underdog in his struggle to knock the braggart off his high horse.

Under the layers of taboos that forbid us to be our natural selves, each of us will find a bit of the braggart we are taught to despise. We tend to disown it in ourselves and disapprove of it in others.

### The Taboo Against Tears

The following discussion between husband and wife about money started calmly but gradually grew into an argument.

**Husband:** I'm tired of talking about it. We're not getting any place. You're just going to have to spend less money and that's all there is to it.

**Wife:** Well, you look at my budget and tell me where I can cut down. I don't buy anything we don't need. I haven't bought anything for the house lately and it's been months since I've bought anything for myself.

**Husband:** That's what you tell me all the time.

**Wife:** (*Becoming more upset*) You make me sound like I'm irresponsible and there's no way I can convince you that I am doing the best I can.

**Husband:** Well, you are irresponsible. If I earned twice what I am making now, I think you'd still manage to spend all of it and justify every penny of it.

**Wife:** (*Bursting into tears*) I don't know what you want me to do. I'll go out and a get a job. Maybe that will satisfy you.

**Husband:** Dammit! Stop crying! Why can't we ever discuss anything without you bawling sooner or later? You know I can't stand your tears. That's always your best weapon. You make me feel like I'm some kind of ogre.

**Wife:** I can't help it. I try not to cry, but I get so frustrated arguing with you that the tears just come.

In their argument the husband reacts to his wife's tears as if she were wrong to allow herself to cry. Expressing emotion of any kind through tears is a perfectly valid human response. The husband's anxiety is really within himself. If he is uncomfortable when his wife cries, most likely he would be even more uncomfortable with his own tears.

**TOXIC MYTH #7**
**The stronger and more mature a person is, the fewer tears he or she sheds — especially he.**

Tears are taboo. Indeed, the taboo against tears is so pervasive that most people are embarrassed by them and try to help someone who is crying *stop* as soon as possible. Yet when we allow ourselves to "have a good cry"—for whatever reason—we usually feel relieved and relaxed afterward—unless we are victims of the taboo against tears. We are taught that tears are childish, that "big boys don't cry." The latter, incidentally, is part of our toxic mythology about differences between the sexes.

There is no human feeling or emotion that, when sufficiently intense, would not naturally be accompanied by tears, yet we associate tears exclusively with pain and frustration. When we see someone overwhelmed with joy on some happy occasion, we usually see them struggling *against* their tears. To make matters worse, those around them may squeeze down their tears also. Such situations usually feel unnatural and awkward. The body wants to shed tears of joy as part of its total expression.

*Tears are an expression of aliveness.* When we hear someone say "I haven't cried in 30 years" or "I never feel like crying," we sense that this person is emotionally dead and probably does not experience or express much feeling of any kind. Such persons respond mechanically and lack the softness and emotional openness of healthy people.

The taboo against tears that says crying is a weakness exemplifies an obsolete attitude that can be traced to our historical past. A hunter in pursuit of a dangerous animal must suppress his fear to satisfy his need for food. A soldier in combat has no time to cry over a fallen comrade if the enemy is approaching. Where crying presents no real handicap or danger, however, it relieves our feelings of distress, so that we are more able to turn our attention to whatever frustrating or disturbing situation demands it.

Each of us has tears of joy and tears of anger. We have tears of sadness and tears of frustration. We have tears of hopelessness, and tears of helplessness. We cry when we are hurt. We cry when we hurt someone else. We cry when we laugh too hard, and we cry when we are exhausted. We cry from pain and tension, and we cry when we feel relieved. We may even cry during or after sexual orgasm.

How is it possible that a human expression of emotion that constantly appears in such a fantastic variety of human experiences can be considered bad, wrong or unnatural?

Because of the taboos against crying, many people learn to use their tears to manipulate others. They learn to cry on cue, and are aware that doing so is often an effective way of persuading others to give them what they want or to restrain others from doing what they don't want. We are most vulnerable to such manipulations when we ritualistically feel we *must* do something when someone is crying, whether we wish to or not, or whether the person crying wants us to or not.

## The Taboo Against Conflict

Because we are such complex organisms with continuously changing needs, we experience a great deal of conflict and the tensions and vacillations conflict brings. Toxic myths about human behavior often imply that we function in a machine-like manner and with machine-like efficiency in performing the *shoulds* expected of us.

This man-as-a-machine concept demands that the enormously complex processes in us be organized to produce a smooth, harmonious flow of decisions and actions in much the same way that a huge computer bank produces answers. This expectation sets the stage for the toxic myths about the need to be conflict-free in our inner feelings and in making choices.

**TOXIC MYTH #8**
**Experiencing conflict, especially the pain of conflict, means there is something wrong with us.**

Conflict is a normal human process that can best be described as a state of tension or ambivalence we experience in the center of our emotional lives and feel primarily in the chest and stomach. When faced with the need to make a decision, we usually try to weigh the facts rationally (our cortex is not unlike a giant computer) and determine what we "should do." The trouble is that intellectual decisions do not necessarily alter our emotional (body) feelings. When the two are at odds, as is quite common, particularly in our personal lives where emotions play a greater role, the conflict remains and may be heightened by our efforts to shove an intellectual decision down our physical throats.

Once again, the antidote is simple but not easy: conflicts resolve themselves on a gut level when we trust our natural problem-solving capabilities. When a genuine resolution of a conflict occurs, it is an emotional reaction in which we *feel* resolved. The intellect is only a part of this larger process. When we accept the human reality that conflict is normal, natural and even healthy, we can cease forcing ourselves to "make up our minds."

**TOXIC MYTH #9**
**Our logical selves are more valuable than our emotional selves.**

The belief that the intellect is really the focal point of a human being's existence is widely held. The cortex, the part of the brain that has to do with intellectual functioning, logical reasoning and rational thought, is considered to be the most important part of ourselves in motivating us and generating a meaning and purpose in living. A typical attitude is that the body is largely a vehicle to provide the support systems necessary to keep the head functioning in good order and to carry out its instructions. This notion often brings with it the prediction that biological evolution will eventually make us into creatures with huge heads and tiny bodies as science and technology replace the need for muscles and movement.

More realistically, emotional feelings (excitement and joy, as well as the human qualities of love, caring, trust, morality) are really experienced in the body, more specifically, in the chest and stomach. This is where we *feel* our aliveness and those qualities that reflect our humanness.

The false truth that the head is the center of an individual's existence fits very well with our technically oriented culture and its emphasis on productivity and accomplishments. The toxic effect of this myth is that it teaches us to devalue our emotional life, or even consider it as a liability, rather than appreciate it as a deeper aspect of our being.

The myth that logic is more valuable than emotions encourages us to suppress our feelings and control those emotions that are considered signs of weakness. Once we worship the intellect as godlike, the process of suppressing our emotional selves seems to follow, as if doing otherwise would hamper efficient mental functioning or be interpreted as a sign of weakness.

While intellectual development is worthwhile, it becomes toxic when we value it more highly than emotional development and fail to realize that the relationship between the two is symbiotic: a rich emotional life stimulates the intellect; a well-developed intellect enables us to give more creative expression to our emotions.

In relating to each other, we must not only think, but *feel*; we must talk and listen from our hearts. Much of the alienation and loneliness people experience within themselves and in relating to others is caused by their functioning exclusively on an intellectual level while deliberately suppressing their aliveness, their feelings.

When we live only in keeping with the dictates of our logical minds, we make our lives drab. We look upon activities that are pleasurable but not productive as a waste of time. We do not allow Beauty to be its own excuse for being. Even the poorest, most materialistically deprived cultures, where people must constantly struggle for physical survival, allow time for holidays and ceremonies designed to stimulate their members emotionally and spiritually so they can experience life more meaningfully.

## TOXIC MYTH #10
## We should be consistent.

The word *but* is an example of the mechanical attitude that distorts the resolution of conflict. It beclouds the true nature of human decision-making. *But* is a refusal to accept the fact that each aspect of a conflict is a valid, legitimate part of ourselves. When we say to someone, "I love you *but* right now I'm so angry I don't want to talk to you," we poison ourselves with the taboo that we shouldn't have conflicting or "inconsistent" feelings.

The word *or* is often a similar manifestation of the taboo against conflict. While the word *but* invalidates part of our conflict, the word *or* reflects the demand that we make up our mind: it says that we have two alternatives from which to choose, that we should accept one and discard (alienate ourselves from) the other.

Decision-making is an ongoing process in which simultaneously existing needs, which are to some degree antagonistic, push for expression through some kind of action. When we do not take a clear stand in a conflict, we are deciding *not* to decide, at least temporarily.

One of the less polite expressions emanating from impatience with indecision is the injunction to "fish or cut bait." This toxic ritual reduces our decision-making processes to an artifact, an unnatural activity rather than one that will evolve spontaneously (believe it or not!) when external and self-imposed internal pressures are not too disruptive. The word *and* is more natural than those words that tend to split us into pieces (*or, but, however,* etc.). *And* is a unifying, integrating word that implies an accepting attitude toward all our feelings and needs—all aspects of ourselves, including our inconsistencies. The word *and* eliminates the judgmental and demanding quality from the decision-making process.

A human being *is* full of inconsistencies, contradictions and ambivalent feelings. With a minimum of awareness and open-mindedness, most people realize that they have numerous antagonistic, contradictory feelings, attitudes and behavior patterns, that all aspects of the self never blend together in total harmony. Myths that reject conflict as part of our humanness hinder our ability to come to terms with the pain of our frustrations.

Most of us do not learn during childhood and adolescence to tolerate the discomfort of anxiety. Toxic myths teach us that anxieties are bad and that we should try to eliminate them as expediently as possible. We learn that anxiety is something we should not have to put up with in the first place, and we feel its presence reflects some personal inadequacy within us.

Because a normal amount of anxiety helps us focus our attention on our emerging needs, those myths that insist we should be consistent and should be able to make decisions easily and rapidly cause unnecessary stress that is often more painful than coping with the frustrations of our unfulfilled needs, an unavoidable fact of life.

**Art:**  (*Role playing, i.e., talking to his mother as if she were actually present*) It's really difficult for me to imagine talking to you because I never could talk to you. I have a lot of bad feelings toward you, the kind I'm not supposed to have. I want to keep you as far away from me as I can. It's hard for me to say it, but I think you never were interested in understanding me and only looked at the results. Keep up a good front, so no one will know.

As soon as I feel angry at you, I rationalize it away, like it's not your fault. I guess you really trained me well. As soon as something comes into my mind—how you hurt me—immediately I cut it off. That it was not your fault. It was the situation you were brought up with. I never got what I needed from you when I was a child, and now I want to insulate myself from you, which is really hard because I have feelings of love for you *at the same time.*

I feel like you are still very important in my life. *But* what prevents me from telling you about my anger is my gratitude. I'm angry at you *but* I don't want to hurt you.

> I have the temptation to say, "You're
> right" or "I'm wrong." What I tried to say
> is that I love you *but* part of you I reject.

**Therapist:** Tell her I love you *and* I reject you.

**Art:** I love you *and* I reject you. I do. I love you
*and* I hate you. I love you *and* sometimes
you are a pain in the ass. That felt nice.

Art is faced with the reality of his ambivalent feelings
toward his mother. The pain that is unnecessary (unrealistic) is centered on his refusal to accept his conflict. And
this was more disturbing to Art than his ambivalent feelings. When he realized that it was all right to experience
inner conflict, he immediately felt relief.

Consistency, when considered a virtue, becomes simply
another toxic ritual ("We should at least try to act consistently"), and inconsistency becomes another toxic taboo.
The consistency myth demands that we resolve our conflicts and contradictory feelings and needs once and for
all. As its victims, we waste our energy erecting a façade
of consistency behind which to hide our ambivalence and
equivocation.

**TOXIC MYTH #11**
**We should be decisive.**

This myth teaches us that decisiveness, like consistency, is
a virtue to be admired while indecisiveness is a personal
failing. Indecisiveness is natural when one conflicting need
is not clearly perceived to be more urgent than another.
When we are not ready to make a choice, indecisiveness
is a natural state of inner conflict and it is naturally uncomfortable. It does not mean that we suffer from some
kind of inadequacy. When we accept the imperative,
"make up your mind," we force ourselves into artificial,

self-manipulative behavior. Decision-making processes evolve in their own way in their own time and cannot be programmed. Adherence to the myth about indecisiveness causes us to victimize ourselves with the toxic ritual of setting deadlines while believing that we are helping—or forcing—ourselves to reach a decision. Such deadline setting disrupts our natural, spontaneous, self-regulating abilities. Individuals who have sufficient self-trust allow whatever time it takes for their decisions to evolve. When we trust this natural process, we don't "make" decisions: the decisions evolve spontaneously and germinate into action without the need for any deliberateness.

Wendy had worked in various managerial positions in several large companies for over 15 years. Her record clearly established her executive ability, and on three occasions other firms had lured her away from her employer by offering her a better position. Finally she applied to yet another company for a job she had always wanted.

Wendy got the job, but her excitement dwindled when she discovered what her new boss was like. He had opposed giving her the position in the first place, but the other executives were convinced that she would be a valuable asset to the company. It was obvious to Wendy that her boss was not going to give her a fair chance. He only begrudgingly delegated to her any kind of authority or decision-making responsibilities. Frequently he would send her out on trivial matters that any file clerk could have taken care of.

Immediately Wendy felt the conflict, and the question of how long to continue trying to establish a more acceptable working relationship with her boss plagued her. She kept hoping that he would finally accept her, but as the months went by his attitude changed very little. Yet she still was unwilling to give up the job. At the same time, she knew that working with this man was intolerable to her.

This conflict went round and round in Wendy's head. Then one Monday morning, after a particularly frustrating weekend, Wendy came to the office and heard some news that was, indeed, the last straw. She learned indirectly that one of her subordinates was being promoted above her.

Prompted by this event, Wendy *finally* came to her decision. All the earlier experiences with her boss, all the thinking about whether or not to quit that had gone on for months, were all part of her decision-making process. Her indecisiveness was at an end! One week later Wendy found another job and gave her notice. She felt genuine relief that she had quit and a great sense of satisfaction with her decision—the satisfaction that comes when we allow our natural decision-making processes to unfold as they will, which usually feels good emotionally as well as intellectually.

## The Taboo Against Mistakes

| | |
|---|---|
| **Marie (age 24):** | I bought a car, Dad, and it's a lemon. I know you told me to buy an American car, but I bought a foreign car and you were right: it's really a lousy car. |
| **Marie's Father:** | God-dammit! Why didn't you listen to me? You know, if you'd just listen to me you wouldn't make such dumb mistakes. |

> **Marie:**  You make me feel terrible. You make me
> feel like you always know the right thing
> to do and I'm an idiot if I make a mistake,
> as if mistakes are inexcusable. I'm not
> supposed to make mistakes. You make me
> feel that if I don't do everything perfect,
> I'll be letting you down.

Marie allows herself to be victimized by the taboo
against making mistakes. She sees her choosing a foreign
car and regretting this decision as a reflection on herself
as a person. ("You make me feel terrible.") The effects of
other toxic myths are also present in Marie's attitude about
her decision. For example, she continues to give over her
power to the authority of her father under the assumption
that he knows better than she even though his knowledge
of cars is no greater than her own. Because he is an authority figure, she values his opinion more than her own. In
addition, she victimizes herself with the taboo against
doing what she really wants to do without having to justify
her decision (i.e., she prefers a foreign car). The irony of
these situations is that if, for instance, Marie had bought
an American car that turned out to be a lemon, she would
most likely not have gotten angry with her father and put
him down in the way she allows him to do to her. It probably would have been considered just bad luck!

This brief dialogue illustrates a typical characteristic of
toxic myths: they come in clusters and in this way their
destructive power is multiplied. Marie violated the taboo
against making mistakes. She violated the taboo against
being indecisive. She allowed herself to be victimized by
the myths that her worth as a person is based on her
ability to make decisions that turn out well, and that her
father, an authority figure, is an expert in everything.

The taboo against mistakes indoctrinates us with the
false notion that it is only results that count and that the
process of learning (growing) is not only secondary but
often considered unimportant. When we become victims

of the taboo against making mistakes, we place enormous pressure on ourselves to perform well (and quickly) in everything we do. This pressure inhibits our willingness to experiment, to try new things. New learning is risky because it does not *always* produce fruitful (successful) results and the self-imposed social and psychological penalties for failure are painfully high.

## TOXIC MYTH #12
**Making mistakes means we are losers.**

Because life includes an unending series of what are commonly called mistakes, it is unfortunate that we are taught that mistakes are bad and shouldn't happen. More realistically, a "mistake" is an experiment that did not turn out as we hoped it would, a reflection of our imperfection, not a measure of our worth.

On the basis of vague inner feelings that we are inadequate or don't do things well enough, we may decide we are making "too many" mistakes and label ourselves "losers." The label becomes a self-fulfilling prophecy. Each new "mistake" confirms our fears that we really *are* "losers." The more convinced we become, the more we expect to fail: no matter how hard we try, nothing ever goes well anyhow.

When we decide to free ourselves from the artificial and unnecessary constrictions that the myths, taboos and rituals discussed here have created to some extent in all of us, we open the gates for the resurgence of our natural abilities to grow toward the full bloom of our unique individual selves. A flood of trapped energy then emerges that can enhance the fullness and meaningfulness of our lives enormously. In adulthood we can begin this process any time we choose to. It is also our ongoing choice when we choose *not* to—the opportunity remains to the last day of our lives. In truth each of us can and will take our freedom only when *we* are ready. When we wait for permission to be free, we wait forever.

Is This
Really
What I Want
To Do
With

My Family Life

## Myths About the Family

Our mythology portrays the family as a source of love, security and strength for all members. Toxic myths about the family reflect a romantic kind of idealism encouraging unreal attitudes about what we have a right to expect from each other because we belong to the same family.

### TOXIC MYTH #13
### Family members must love each other.

We are taught not only that family members love each other now, but that they always will. On this basis, we then project our personal expectations onto each member of the family. There are, of course, deep love relationships within practically all families that survive and grow in spite of the normal and inevitable conflicts, rivalries and hostilities. The physical and emotional intimacy of living together and knowing each other so well can enhance this love, and this is what we are taught to expect. But it can also destroy it!

Feelings of love are not static: they evolve according to how the members of a family relate to each other. Within the family constellation of parents and children, individual personalities of family members and their experiences with each other become increasingly relevant as children grow older. As children enter early adolescence, family interaction will determine how the love family members have for each other will be manifested, or whether a pattern of alienation will emerge. After they reach adulthood, many persons continue for the rest of their lives to relate to their families out of a sense of duty. This kind of interaction is so often an empty ritual that serves largely to absolve feelings of guilt. Such so-called "giving" only creates more resentment on the part of the giver (which is usually taboo) and further diminishes the possibilities for spontaneous, caring interaction. Family get-togethers then become more obviously formal ritual, and the lack of real closeness and caring also becomes more apparent.

Most people are by now quite aware of the increasing breakdown of the traditional bonds of love, loyalty and closeness within the family. Some authorities even believe that the traditional family unit is unnecessary. Others feel that any variance from the traditional patriarchy will create disobedient children and broken homes. Such drastic and chaotic attitudes exemplify the destructive influence of clinging to toxic myths and trying to live according to their absolute rituals and taboos.

New and more realistic family interactions are needed. The dictatorial power of authoritarian parents—fathers in particular—is out of step with the changing nature of relationships in our society. Most obviously, with the emergence of feminism, women are less willing to accept traditional subservient roles. Similarly, children feel a sense of growing power and have discovered that they can rebel more openly and effectively against manipulation by the adult world.

When we are willing to face this new reality, the antidote would call for an attitude change in which the integrity of each member of the family is fully recognized and respected. In family interactions, this means giving up expectations that other members of the family think and act as we think they ought to. This antidote also requires we recognize that no one owes us love, and that trying to demand it is toxic—and won't work anyhow.

Similarly, the antidote based on genuine respect for the integrity of others requires minimizing the use of parental power and punishment in establishing the necessary limits and rules for behavior and interaction within the family.

Finally, a most effective antidote is achieved when we accept the harsh reality that, in intimate relationships, nobody owes us anything. While the latter is hard to swallow (or even accept as valid), it can be enormously effective in minimizing the many ways family members intrude on each other with demands and expectations.


**TOXIC MYTH #14**
**We should enjoy being with family**
**members more than we enjoy being with**
**our friends.**

This myth makes the normal love among members of a family into a demand. In many families, it is taboo for children to tell their parents they would rather be with their friends than with their family. The same taboo applies to parents. They too are apt to hide their feelings when they want to get away from their children. Often the resulting guilt feelings are devastating.

|  |  |
|---|---|
| **Bobby**<br>**(age four):** | Why do you and Daddy have to go out? Why can't you stay home and be with me? I get scared when you're not here. |
| **Mother:** | Well, we won't be out late and I'll come in and kiss you when I get home. We promised our friends that we would be there and we don't want to disappoint them. Daddy and I will be home tomorrow night and the babysitter will take good care of you while we're gone tonight. |

In this dialogue, the mother's response to her child's demands is to give excuses. Furthermore, she is essentially evasive, as she doesn't really answer Bobby's questions. The guilt she experiences for wanting to go out with her husband and leave Bobby home is also implicit in her need to make atonement by promising to stay home the next night. An antidote to this dilemma would be to give Bobby a simple, more honest answer:

> **Mother:** I understand how you feel and I know you would rather have us stay home. When Daddy and I go out to visit our friends, it's a kind of play time that we need. It's just like when you want to go to a birthday party at your friend's house.

Family myths, taboos and rituals about togetherness imply that we should want to spend as much time as possible with our family and that "togetherness" contributes to a family's healthy emotional development. Some parents carry this ritual to the point of not allowing one of their children to go out and play with friends unless the child is willing to take a younger brother or sister along! Or parents themselves act as if it is taboo for one of them to enjoy activities, particularly outside the home, without the other.

When we regulate our behavior mechanically according to such myths, our resentments grow and we learn more devious ways to get away and stay away. Families may sit together for hours in front of a television set sharing nothing but superficial conversation—and very little of that. Fostering more intimate bonds within the family requires a mutual desire, rather than an enforced rule, to be together. The *quality* of such interaction is far more important than the amount of time spent together or the specific activity shared.

## Myths About Parents and Parenthood

Young children normally perceive their parents as all-powerful and all-knowing. This mythical attitude persists as part of our culture, and many of our rituals and taboos serve to shore up the prestige and authority of parenthood.

### TOXIC MYTH #15
### Father knows best.

Parents themselves, and fathers in particular, cling to the myth that, because they are the child's parents and are older and more experienced, their personal views and opinions should always be considered as more valid than their children's. Furthermore, ritual demands that their children, even in adulthood, should continue to accept this myth, which only aggravates the inevitable strife between parent and child as children grow older.

### TOXIC MYTH #16
### Wisdom comes with age.

While it does require time to discover and assimilate knowledge about what the world and life are like, becoming wise is quite another matter and largely depends on *how* we integrate our experiences and what attitudes and actions are forthcoming from them. Being older than someone else, especially within the family, more frequently brings rigidity and dogmatism and results in an unthinking attempt by the old to force their attitudes, beliefs and opinions on the young.

**Father:**   I don't care how many of your friends are going camping, you're not going.

**Daughter:**   You treat me like I'm a baby! I'm 17 years old!

**Father:**   Yeah, you're 17, and already you think you know it all! You don't know what the world is like! You think you can just sleep on a beach someplace and nobody's going to bother you, huh?

**Daughter:**   All my friends are going. There are 12 of us. We're going to a state park where they've got campsites and a park ranger.

**Father:**   I don't care about that. You still need adult supervision. You think I want to keep you from having a good time? I just know that bad things could happen, and I'm trying to protect you until you find out what the world is really like.

**Daughter:**   How am I going to find out what the world is like when you and Mom hover over me like I'm a three-year-old?

**Father:**   See, that's what I mean. You can't even have a discussion without a temper tantrum. When you get older, you'll learn your Dad knew a lot more than you thought he did. Then you'll appreciate me.

**Daughter:**   Sometimes when you talk to me like that I really feel like splitting.

In this dialogue, the father continues to use his parental power even though he is alienating his daughter in the process. Parents often dump their anxiety on their children rather than dealing with it within themselves, where it belongs. Most parents do, of course, worry about their children. It is quite another matter when they prohibit them from experimenting and learning about life not because of the realistic limitations on the freedom they allow their children, but because of their (the parent's) own anxieties and fears.

This dialogue also exemplifies how myths are perpetuated by each new generation. For now, the daughter is the victim, but she is also learning the power of the taboo against violating parental authority so that, when she becomes a parent and feels fearful and anxious as her children assert themselves, she can in turn, use the power of the toxic myths about parenthood, with their accompanying taboos and rituals, to control her children.

## TOXIC MYTH #17
### We can learn about life by listening to others.

Many parents sincerely believe that relating their own experiences can spare their children the pains of growing up, making their own mistakes and discovering for themselves how to get along in the world. The myth that age brings wisdom and that this wisdom can be transferred verbally to the young usually takes the form of a ritual in which an older authority figure lectures to a younger person over whom he or she has control, at least temporarily. Parents often continue their lecturing and advice-giving (known to the young as "nagging") so as if by sheer repetition their message will eventually sink in and their reluctant victims will finally acknowledge their wisdom.

**TOXIC MYTH #18**
**A good mother never resents her children.**

This myth is a source of endless guilt for millions of mothers in our society who feel stress and frustration as they try to meet the constant demands of their young children. Yet when mothers feel resentful, they also feel guilty.

The taboo against mothers' resenting their own children is doubly toxic because many mothers believe these unacceptable feelings of resentment and guilt must be kept secret. The truth, of course, is that these repressed feelings may find their expression in physical or verbal child abuse, a phenomenon that is apparently widespread in our society.

**TOXIC MYTH #19**
**Rearing healthy children is a complex problem.**

The number of books, articles and lectures on child-rearing is more a reflection of our unrealistic anxiety than that we need so much knowledge and advice on how to raise children.

Many parents who have little or no knowledge of modern child psychology manage to rear emotionally healthy children with a minimum of anxiety. These parents have a basic respect for the integrity of their children from the time they are born and enough self-trust to follow their own intuition in relating to them.

## Myths About Marriage

**TOXIC MYTH #20**
**Marriage promises a new way of life.**

Our traditional romantic myths about love and marriage continue to have an almost mystical quality. They teach us that getting married is the beginning of a new way of life that should mean that many of the frustrations and dissatisfactions with ourselves and our way of living prior to marriage should greatly diminish or be alleviated altogether. Myths about marriage lead us to believe that, if we have failed to find single life satisfying and gratifying, or if we feel overwhelmed by our emotional conflict, anxieties and insecurities, falling in love and getting married will provide a rich, new source of help and assistance. ("After all, now that I have a partner, it's got to be easier!") Marriage myths imply that, when two persons choose to share their lives, the simple fact of their being together divides the chores of living so that each can now expect life to be only half the problem it was before. The idea that marriage will resolve personal emotional conflicts and psychic pains is another version of the myth that someone else can cope with life for us, can do for us what we have been unable (or unwilling) to do for ourselves.

The marriage-is-a-way-of-life myth also teaches us that the only prerequisite for living happily ever after is mutual love. This myth fosters an attitude making it taboo for a couple contemplating marriage to *really* face their resentments toward each other and confront each other with them. Instead, most people ritualistically rationalize or in other ways avoid open confrontation about various attitudes, beliefs or behavior that could be destructive to their marriage. They think to themselves but seldom say, "After we're married, I'll change that in him (her)." The corollary assumption is also often made: "After we're married and *because* we love each other, each will change in whatever way is necessary to please the other."

This ritualistic attitude about love and marriage usually operates as follows: "If you really loved me you would . . . ."

The last part of this sentence has a thousand variations, all toxic, for example: . . . talk to me more; . . . not get angry with me; . . . be nicer to my parents; . . . give me more sex; . . . give up drinking; . . . not play golf so much; . . . have dinner ready when I get home.

This way of relating uses love to manipulate the other person. When conflicts arise, the real issues of recognizing that differences in needs and consequent dissatisfactions of many kinds are part of any intimate relationship gets lost in these expectations that toxic myths about love and marriage have, since childhood, taught us to believe. This myth that love conquers all—or should—continues to be a major source of terrible disruption in intimate, one-to-one relationships.

**TOXIC MYTH #21**
**If two people love each other, they can**
**solve any conflict that may arise between**
**them.**

The first round of the "love conquers all" myth often begins with the "thunder and lightening" experience of a new relationship, which fills the couple with excitement and joy. When, as inevitably happens, the initial enchantment of their new relationship begins to wane and conflicts begin to occur, the toxic effect of our romantic myths about love and their disillusionment lead the couple to conclude: "You don't love me any more. If you did we wouldn't be having these problems!"

Toxic myths in general tend to make us deaf, dumb and blind. In this instance, we fail to see that, although the marriage relationship can provide the deep satisfactions of loving and feeling loved, each person brings to the relationship his or her respective patterns of "hang-ups" to which are now added the inevitable and unpredictable complications that inevitably arise when two human beings live together. Although most of us would acknowledge arguments are inevitable, romantic myths continue to perpetuate the belief that marital conflict is something not only to resolve but it can be put to an end. According to the "love conquers all myth," when two "mature" people have established a "mature" relationship this precludes any real conflict between them.

## TOXIC MYTH #22
**By getting married and being part of a family, we can avoid the anxieties and fears of learning to live with ourselves.**

John and Mary had been living together for about a year when the following dialogue occurred:

> **John:** Living with you is getting to be a pain. Lately you're always depressed or irritated about something. I love you, but your bitchiness is really beginning to get to me.
>
> **Mary:** Well, you're not any fun anymore either. I'm bored sitting around every night while you drink beer and watch that damned TV all night long. There's got to be more to life than this. We come home from work. I fix dinner while you read the paper. Then we sit around all night hardly even talking to each other. I'd like to go out, have some fun, have some friends over or do some-

thing to break the monotony. I know I'm getting bitchy and I don't like it any more than you do, but there must be more to life than just living together like this.

**John:** Okay, I'll level with you. I resent you having lunch with John even if he is just a good friend. I really feel irritated when you tell me what kind of interesting conversations the two of you have. So I figure the hell with it if you want to go out with him, fine. But I'll be damned if I'll take you out when you give him so much attention.

**Mary:** We just like rapping with each other. Every time I suggest inviting him and his wife over, you turn that down, too. You're the man I love, but I think we both need more than our relationship with each other. And I really resent your punishing me, not talk- to me or taking me any place just because you resent my being with my friends.

**John:** Okay. You know I feel insecure about whether people like me and I find it hard to make friends. But I know my getting even with you this way isn't fair either.

**Mary:** That's right and these arguments are driving us apart. I think we need to sit down together and see what we can do to improve our relationship. Maybe it would help if we get married. Then you might feel more secure about us.

**John:** Well, I'm afraid you'll find someone else more exciting. Maybe getting married would help.

**Mary:**   I really didn't think you would consider marriage. I'm excited about this and I also feel closer to you than I have in months.

**John:**   You know, I feel excited, too! Okay, let's set a date for the wedding. At least our families will be pleased. That's for sure!

## TOXIC MYTH #23
**Getting married is a way to resolve conflicts in a relationship.**

Like many myths, this one has a grain of truth in that marriage is a statement of mutual commitment between two people. In that sense it can strengthen the bonds between two people and add new dimensions to their relationship. When a couple believes, however, the myth that the act of getting married is in itself a solution to their conflicts, it can be more destructive than helpful. The myth may cause them to have unrealistic expectations that simply getting married will resolve their differences or ensure that their relationship will grow and become more mutually nourishing. When a couple marries as a solution to existing problems, it sets the stage for the emergence of other toxic myths, for example, the obsolete notion that, because they are now husband and wife, they each have a right to expect a greater responsiveness than existed between them previously. The toxic myths about marriage have this underlying character: that two people *owe* each other (and will provide) more giving and caring than they were experiencing previously. This is the kind of toxic attitude that marriage myths still convey and so contribute to the high divorce rate in our society.

John and Mary's plan to marry is their way of trying to reverse a deteriorating relationship. It is nothing more than a manipulation of themselves and each other despite their good intentions. The poisonous effect of the marriage myths is the belief that the act of marriage will change how they relate to each other. It is more likely that it will serve temporarily to cover up the real underlying differences in their needs and individual personalities, which are not going to change simply because they become husband and wife.

When John and Mary agreed to marry, they felt an initial elation and excitement. Their feelings of love for each other blossomed as during the early months of their relationship. The plans and activities surrounding their forthcoming marriage seemed to melt away their conflicts and frustrations. After their marriage they enjoyed a blissful honeymoon period. Initially, John became more sociable and more interested in sharing activities with Mary and she, in turn, felt more in love with him than ever. Gradually, the impetus and momentum of their "new life together" began to wane. They both became aware that their old resentments and frustrations with each other were emerging again. They were at the point of talking about divorce when Mary unexpectedly became pregnant.

## TOXIC MYTH #24
### Having children is a way to resolve conflicts in a deteriorating marriage.

After initially considering abortion, John and Mary used the same attitude about having a baby that they did about getting married. They agreed that a child would be a way of creating a new bond between them and renewing the intimacy and closeness that were again on the wane. According to this popular myth, sharing the joys and tribulations of bringing a child into the world would bring them closer together—now that they would both be responsible for another human being.

This time it was only a matter of a few months before they both realized that they had been victimized by their belief in this popular myth. The added stress the baby placed on them was soon apparent. Mary felt frustrated about having to give up her professional activities, while John felt resentment and jealousy because of the demands the baby placed on Mary. Again, despite their good intentions, the basis on which they had decided to have a baby was a manipulation; that is, they hoped the baby would be "useful" in saving their marriage. They expected the baby to do what they could or would not.

**TOXIC MYTH #25**
**Mutual parental responsibility toward**
**children enhances the love and intimacy**
**between husband and wife.**

Both John and Mary were well-meaning people and felt a strong sense of responsibility toward their child. Both were sincere in wanting to work through their problems and keep their family together. Nevertheless, their resentments and the differences between their needs, plus the demands and added restrictions that came with having a baby, only intensified the deterioration of their intimacy. Their financial problems worsened with their new expenses and the loss of Mary's income. Both John and Mary became increasingly irritable, often snapping at each other at the slightest provocation. This in turn led to a deterioration of their sexual relationship. Their relationship eroded into the not too uncommon pattern of a husband and wife living under the same roof. John and Mary felt no more closeness than boarders in a rooming house. When the baby was three years old, Mary found a day-care facility and resumed her career. Six months later, she filed for divorce.

Myths about the cohesiveness of the family are often obsolete when they originated during past eras when families literally had to stay together for economic and other practical reasons are often obsolete today. To believe that getting married or bearing children will maintain a man-woman relationship or sustain the family unit in the face of deteriorating intimacy is simply to be victimized by yet another toxic myth. In contrast, nourishing attitudes towards marriage and family are based on a couple wanting to share a common life-style in and of itself, rather than for some particular motive or goal they hope to achieve through these means.

## TOXIC MYTH #26
## Even a bad marriage is healthier for children than a divorce.

According to this toxic myth, John and Mary tried to stay together for the sake of their child. They were strongly reinforced in this endeavor by both families who adhered to the traditional view that anything is better for a child than *not* living with both parents. In this respect, it is significant that their baby developed a variety of allergies and illnesses during the three years that John and Mary remained together. They discounted their physician's comment that the emotional stress between them might be contributing to the child's problems. As it turned out, following their separation, the child's illnesses and allergies rapidly diminished.

## Thou Shalt Answer All Questions

There is a strict taboo against children's refusing to answer questions even if they are trite, too personal, or downright intrusive. As adults, most people continue the ritual that, when asked a question, one should answer. To respond with "I don't wish to answer your question" violates this ritual and is apt to be taken as a personal affront by the questioner. The question-and-answer ritual is instilled in childhood, and it is a rare adult who respects a child's right to refuse to answer questions. "What's your name?" "What do you like to do?" "What do you want to be when you grow up?" "Who's your best friend?" etc., etc. Such a series of questions even when put to the child by a total stranger, typically elicits an embarrassed, apologetic response from the parents when their child, finger in mouth, stares curiously as he or she silently ignores the interrogator. Without some kind of social coercion we, as adults, would frequently and quite naturally not respond to this type of question-and-answer ritual. Children sense their parents' anxiety that they are not meeting their expectations and in turn become anxious and disturbed. Most adults continue to ignore their reluctance to respond to interrogations especially in areas of their personal life, where it is no one's business in the first place. Instead, we learn to be evasive, trite, clever, or to lie—anything, so long as we don't openly defy the ritual.

> **Wife:** (*Angry because her husband came home an hour late for dinner without letting her know*) Why couldn't you call and let me know you were going to be an hour late? Why can't you excuse yourself from what-

ever you're doing and make a two-minute phone call?

**Husband:** We had an important sales conference. I thought it would end early and I would be home at the usual time. We got into some very heated issues and I didn't want to walk out in the middle.

**Wife:** You always forget about me here waiting for you, wondering what happened. Why can't you be more considerate?

**Husband:** There were 20 people there, including my bosses, and I just couldn't get up in the middle of some important policy-making decisions and interrupt everybody to go out and make a phone call.

**Wife:** You mean these people you work with are more important than me?

**Husband:** Of course not! I just didn't feel it was appropriate. Sometimes I'm not going to be able to let you know I'll be late.

**Wife:** (*Still angry*) Is that your idea of marriage?

**Husband:** Most of the people there are married. No one else got up to make a phone call. I would have been annoyed if anyone else had gotten up in the middle of everything to make some phone call no matter what the reason was.

**Wife:** Don't you care about my feelings? Is this how you show your love for me?

In this typical question-and-answer ritual, the husband keeps trying to defend himself, to explain his behavior and justify his actions to his wife. While a statement or two about what happened that had caused him to be late is reasonable, the dialogue deteriorates into a futile interrogation. The husband seeks to satisfy his wife by getting her to see the episode his way and refusing to allow her to continue to see it her way. He is unwilling to accept her anger and resentment and allow her to have her own emotional reaction and instead ritualistically answers her every question. In the following dialogue, the husband does not allow himself to be manipulated into a question-and-answer ritual:

**Wife:** What in the world happened to you? I was really getting worried.

**Husband:** I had an important sales conference and it went on much longer than I had anticipated. We had to finish what we were doing. I'm sorry I was late.

**Wife:** I really resent you when you're an hour late for dinner and you don't let me know. I don't think that your explanation is at all satisfactory.

**Husband:** I know you're angry. I've told you what happened. I'm really sorry I upset you but it couldn't be helped. I don't care for your interrogations.

**Wife:** You're not going to get away that easy. Yes, I am still angry and I want a more satisfactory explanation. Why can't you arrange your meetings earlier in the day?

**Husband:** I'm not going to answer any more questions. I've said all I care to.

> **Wife:**    How do I even know you won't start doing this every day?
>
> **Husband:**    (*Husband doesn't answer.*)
>
> **Wife:**    Why don't you answer?
>
> **Husband:**    I'm going to take a walk.

It always takes two to play games, including those that reflect various toxic taboos and rituals. Rarely can such situations be cleared up to the satisfaction of both people. When the husband takes a stand and stops the futile effort to provide satisfactory answers, it leaves his wife frustrated. This also increases the possibility that she might find a more satisfactory way to work through her frustration. As long as both play the question-answer ritual, the conflict is stalemated and both remain frustrated by continuing to be caught up in their endless game.

No two marriage situations or experiences create the same set of circumstances. The myths that govern and control marriage problems are only as effective as their recipients want them to be. If we are aware of the toxic effect that many of these traditional myths can have on a relationship, we can approach each situation and each interaction without preconceived ideas that have no meaning in today's world. To do so we must be capable of recognizing these myths for what they are. Many start in early childhood with comments and suggestions that are now in our subconscious, yet they are myths that control our lives without our knowing or even wanting to participate.

## Childhood: The Helpless Victim

### GET 'EM WHILE THEY'RE YOUNG
Pam is a somewhat precocious four-year-old who is left in the care of a housekeeper because both of her parents

work. At breakfast one morning the following dialogue occurred between Pam and the housekeeper:

**Pam:** *(Addressing housekeeper)* I had a really scarey dream last night. I wish mommy was here because I'm still scared. I dreamed that some big monster was chasing me and I couldn't get away from him.

**Housekeeper:** It serves you right. Children have bad dreams only when they misbehave and have bad thoughts. Maybe now you'll learn to mind me when your folks are gone. God has a way of punishing children who don't behave and you were really a bad little girl yesterday. You didn't eat your breakfast and I had to call you three times when you were out playing. Now you just watch and see. If you behave yourself, you won't have these bad dreams.

For a four-year-old, any adult is an authority figure and whatever one says is apt to be believed. In this instance, Pam continued to have nightmares and would question the housekeeper because she had indeed become extremely well behaved. The housekeeper's response was that Pam was still being punished and that God would decide when it was enough and at that point Pam would no longer have her bad dreams. This example also typifies the myth that parents and adults are all-knowing and that their word is not to be questioned. The housekeeper indoctrinated Pam with this myth for her own purposes so that her job would be easier. This exemplifies the payoff that is always inherent for those who indoctrinate others with various toxic myths.

Furthermore, the housekeeper established her own power over Pam and in this way created an atmosphere in which it was increasingly easy for her to manipulate Pam with various other myths. As the housekeeper's power grew, Pam's fear also grew until it reached a point where the housekeeper began to make Pam swear that she would not discuss any of this with her parents, threatening her that doing so would result in even worse nightmares than she had had before.

The vulnerability of the young child sets the stage for the development of a whole pattern of beliefs that are accepted at face value from adults because of experiences such as the one described above. It easily becomes too threatening for a young child to even question any new kind of indoctrination because of these kinds of frightening experiences.

Endeavors to influence our attitudes and beliefs, as well as *how* we think about human problems, are far more powerful during our childhood years. The earlier this indoctrination begins, the more effective its results are apt to be. Ignorance, powerlessness and susceptibility to believing everything any adult tells us are unavoidable aspects of childhood. To be a child means to be extremely susceptible and defenseless to external pressures from the all-powerful adult world.

**The ability of toxic myths to poison our natural growth and well-being stems from the fact that in childhood we are helpless victims of their destructive power.**

### GUILT, SHAME AND FEAR
Inducing feelings of guilt, shame and fear is the principal method we use with and against children to instill in them

attitudes and behavior that are unnatural, unnecessary and therefore toxic. The adult world typically sends messages that what is "good" is not necessarily similar to how the child would naturally think, feel and act; hence, guilt, shame and fear tactics are necessary to instill toxic myths into our children, and they work. Their poisonous effect, while often subtle, can scarcely be overemphasized. They instill a basic attitude that we are untrustworthy and need this kind of pressure to learn how to live together and behave decently.

George was a bright seven-year-old who lived with his parents and maternal grandmother. Because his parents worked, the grandmother kept house and looked after George when he came home from school. As the only child living with three adults, George received a great deal of affection; however, his grandmother had an expression she would use whenever George misbehaved or in some way caused her to worry. Hardly a day went by when George didn't hear this expression from his grandmother: "Honestly, George, you'll be the death of me yet!" His grandmother had used this expression all her life and did not say it with any particular anger when expressing her frustration with George's typical boyish misbehavior.

While the school George attended was only three blocks away, his grandmother would always watch the clock and worry if he were more than five minutes late getting home. One day as George was returning home from school, a fire engine came roaring by and stopped only a block from his home— an automobile was in flames. George stopped to watch the excitement and was almost an hour late before he realized that his grandmother would be worried.

When George arrived home, he found his grandmother on the floor unconscious. He ran to a neighbor who called an ambulance. His grandmother had suffered a stroke and died a few days later.

George was beside himself with grief and developed an extreme sense of guilt. He could hear his grandmother's words ringing in his ears ("George, you will be the death of me yet!") and began to feel personally responsible for her death.

His parents tried to reassure him that his grandmother was quite old and had had strokes in the past. None of this had any effect in relieving George's overwhelming sense of guilt. He became sullen and quiet, refused to play with his friends, and would go straight to his room after school each day. He began to ask his parents to punish him. He would frequently beg his father to give him a spanking and began refusing the usual treats his parents had given him in the past, saying, "Grandmother was right and I didn't listen to her and now she is dead. I need to be punished. I don't deserve anything good." Such expressions were frequently heard by George's parents. George's parents decided to seek professional help. Despite the weekly sessions with a psychologist, George developed a pattern of rituals and compulsions. When each of his parents would come home he would insist that they tell him exactly six times: "You are a good boy and I love you." On occasion they refused to comply with the ritual and George would become hysterical until they did so.

A new crisis occurred when George's mother became ill with a mild case of the flu. George was absolutely panicked and refused to go to school. He insisted on being with his mother and begged her not to die. Again, there was no way to reassure him that her illness was minor and that she would recover in a few days. She recovered, but George's problem continued. After a year of therapy, George's compulsive pattern began to subside and he gradually began to return to a normal pattern of living. Even then he would frequently panic when his parents or others expressed annoyance with him. This pattern continued well into his high school years. It was only as a young adult that he finally accepted the irrational nature of his guilt and to again feel that he was a worthwhile, loveable human being.

**Irrational guilt, shame and fear make us easy prey to countless toxic myths, taboos and rituals.**

They teach us the lie that we need to be controlled primarily by external authorities, as if there are "evils" within us that must be subdued. This is not based on anything we have done, yet we are taught that we, and our fellow humans, are inherently irresponsible and immoral. This childhood indoctrination makes us vulnerable to similar poison from all the toxic myths, taboos and rituals that flourish in a social climate that teaches us that there is "good" behavior and "bad" behavior, "good" thoughts and "bad" thoughts, "good" feelings and "bad" feelings, and ultimately "good" people and "bad" people. Guilt, shame and fear myths teach us that we are "bad."

## AUTOMATIC NO-NO'S

Each of us learns from a variety of toxic myths that become so deeply ingrained by the time we reach adulthood that a pattern of thoughts, feelings and actions is formed that are labeled automatic no-no's (taboos). Yet every child experiences them despite having been taught these feelings are intrinsically wrong, e.g., anger at one's parents. The emotional power of the taboos that are thrust upon the young child is often so devastating that even in adulthood we continue to accept them submissively, for the child is also taught that it is taboo to ever question or challenge their validity.

Automatic no-no's ignore the reality of normal childhood attitudes, feelings and behavior. Taboos are the inhibitory reactions and prohibitions stemming from the various toxic myths. The taboos that follow illustrate the actual workings of a toxic myth. A myth is somewhat like a law in that it is abstract: we can only know it intellectually, while taboos are what we can experience in living. Taboos and rituals represent toxic mythology in action.

**Mother:**   (*Addressing her son Larry, age 10*) Your father and I want to have a talk with you. We are getting sick and tired of your attitude around the house. I think the way you treat your little brother is awful. He likes you so much and you always seem irritated with him.

**Larry:**   He makes me mad. Sometimes I am talking to you and he comes rushing into the room and interrupts me. Then you turn your attention to him and I have to wait to finish what I want to talk to you about.

**Father:**   I guess you don't remember how it was

when you were four years old. Jimmy's impatient. He comes rushing in and he doesn't see that we are talking and he needs our attention right away. You're older. Why can't you learn to wait?

**Larry:** I do wait, but it bothers me. I don't see why you can't tell Jimmy you're busy until we get done.

**Mother:** Really! You sound like you resent your own brother. You ought to be ashamed of yourself.

**Larry:** (*Starting to get upset with tears coming to his eyes*) You make me feel like you love him more than me. Sometimes I wish he wasn't around at all."

**Father:** (*Getting angry*) Now don't start getting disrespectful or we'll end this conversation right here. Your mother and I are trying to be reasonable and we want to have your cooperation.

**Larry:** (*Now sobbing as he talks*) You've always told me that you want me to come to you and tell you when something is troubling me. I'm telling you that Jimmy is bugging me. I can't help it, he makes me angry.

**Mother:** (*Now also getting exasperated*) How dare you talk that way to us. What kind of upbringing will people think you're getting? Jimmy is not some kid living down the street, he's your brother and you must love him. Maybe we have been too nice and you are just becoming one of those spoiled kids!

**Larry:** (*Trying to control his crying*) You don't understand me. You think Jimmy's just a little angel and I'm always the bad one. I can't help it if I get mad when he hits me or throws something at me. Then he runs to you and I get scolded because I am angry at him. I never see you scolding him like you do me.

**Mother:** Jimmy doesn't talk to us like you do. You'd better learn to button your lip, young man, if you know what's good for you. I think your father and I should talk about what kind of punishment you deserve for the way you are acting right now.

**Father:** Your mother is right. And I don't want you bothering Jimmy. You're too big for that. I don't expect you to hit him when he does something to make you mad. He can't really hurt you, he's only four years old.

**Larry:** Can't you at least tell him to stay out of my room? He gets away with everything and I get all the blame. You never want to see my side of things. You love him more than you do me. I'm just not going to talk to you about anything anymore!

(*Larry runs out of the house crying and ignoring his parents' shouts that he come back at once.*)

The attitude of Larry's parents reflects their adherence, whether they are aware of it or not, to various toxic taboos. The most obvious Larry violated in this dialogue are:

- the taboo against resenting siblings,
- the taboo against challenging parental demands,
- the taboo against feeling anger or hatred toward a loved one,
- the taboo against disliking any member of one's family, and
- the taboo against feeling distrust toward someone you love—especially a parent.

Such taboos are particularly toxic because children experience these feelings frequently while, at the same time, their emotional security and the growth of their self-esteem and self-love require that they feel loved and accepted, particularly by their parents.


**TOXIC MYTH #27**
**If we feel a need for privacy, we are**
**being unfriendly or hostile—especially**
**to people we live with.**


**THE TABOO AGAINST SECRETS**
It is not surprising that the guilt-shame-fear constellation of toxic myths, when pitted against our relentless urges for self-expression and naturalness, makes liars of us all. At the same time it is, of course, taboo for a child to lie or to call anyone he loves a liar. This places the child in a double bind: he is not allowed the right to an inner privacy, while at the same time he knows that what he is thinking or feeling is something that will meet with parental disapproval.

*It is taboo for children to keep secrets from their parents.*
The ritual that comes with this taboo is a seemingly open attitude that the child can tell his or her parents anything

with the assurance of being understood and that there will be no repercussions or punishment. Yet most children learn very early that such expressions invariably meet with some kind of disapproval whether openly in the form of punishment or anger, or where the child simply senses the parental disapproval while the parent struggles to suppress his or her impulse to punish or reprimand. In any case, children are rarely fooled by such maneuvers. To avoid such threatening conflict with the parents, a child will often resort to lies. On the most innocuous level, these are lies of omission. The child simply denies that there is anything bothering him and insists that everything is okay. This creates an additional bind, as it is taboo to lie to one's parents. Thus, a vicious cycle is created, with its increasingly destructive effects.

**THE DOUBLE STANDARD**
Parental rules regarding secrets and lying are quite different from those we typically teach our children. Parents usually have no reservations in deciding what they choose to share or withhold from their children. It cannot be overemphasized that a child invariably senses what is happening within the family unit and what kinds of overt or covert goings-on are occurring, even if he does not know the content of these events. This double standard, itself an act of deception on the part of parents, only serves to generate further anxiety and distrust within the child.

*It is considered an act of love and caring when parents conceal things from their children even when it concerns the children.* This is simply another of the many versions of the attitude: "Don't do as I do, do as I say." The natural consequences of this kind of double standard are distrust of authority and confusion and anxiety about one's self and one's expected role. The increasing freedom that children experience as they grow into adulthood then becomes more a matter of what their increasing power enables them to get away with in the face of authority. They do not learn that freedom includes taking responsibility for one's own behavior; for the more we try to control the behavior of people through fear of punishment, the less each individual is enabled to develop into what would generally be considered a responsible citizen, based on his or her values and inner sense of right and wrong.

## THE TABOO AGAINST OPENNESS
The taboo against secrets has its corollary in the taboo against openness. The taboo against openness is an attempt to exclude from the experience of the child those areas of reality adults consider forbidden. Typically, adults try to act as if these taboo areas don't even exist.

*The alternative to openness is to lie.* Usually these are lies of omission or evasiveness. With the best of intentions the adult world tries to conceal the truth from children. Uncle George (who died) is away on a long trip. Mommy and Daddy don't fight; we love each other (as if the two are mutually exclusive). Or, sex is natural and healthy *but* you're too young to know about it. Nevertheless, when children tell lies, their parents are shocked: "How *could* you lie to your own parents!"

## THE TABOO AGAINST PRIVACY:
## WHAT ARE YOU CHILDREN UP TO?

## TOXIC MYTH #28
**If you loved me, you would want to tell me everything.**

From early childhood, privacy, like secrecy, is taboo: "If you're not up to something bad, why do you want the door closed?" The same question is, of course, taboo for the child to ask of his parents. Privacy is taboo, especially toward our parents. Parents are often hurt or even outraged when they question their children and are given glib answers or no answer at all.

In adulthood, this myth carries over into intimate relationships. We often feel hurt when a loved one openly states that he or she is not willing to share something.

**He:** I'm going to the den. I want to be by myself.

**She:** Are you angry with me? Have I done something to displease you? What's wrong? I want you to share it with me.

**He:** It doesn't have anything to do with you. I want to be alone for a while.

**She:** Well, what good is our marriage if you're not willing to share your troubles with me. If something is bothering you, I have a right to know about it. Maybe I can help.

**He:** I want to be by myself and I want to handle this situation on my own.

**She:** Well, that's just fine. You just do that. I'm going to a movie.

## WITHDRAWAL

Especially in marriage, we dare not openly violate the "togetherness" ritual. Instead, we find more subtle (devious) ways of withdrawing that allow us to avoid directly expressing our need for privacy. For example, having an argument is often a good excuse in order to subsequently withdraw to satisfy one's need for privacy.

Toxic myths give the nod of social approval to the outgoing person, while those who prefer solitude tend to be either frowned upon or merely tolerated. Parents smile approvingly when their children tell them of their social successes. Their attitude is nourishing in that they encourage the child's needs for contact and relating. Parents tend to behave in a toxic manner when a child expresses the opposite needs—wants to be alone and does not want to be sociable. Often, parents ritualistically rationalize such needs: "He's probably not feeling well. . . . He's in a bad mood. Maybe he had a fight with one of his friends." Frequently, their disapproval takes the form of ritualistic questioning, which implies to the child that something must be wrong or he or she would not want to be alone.

Parents seldom convey the balanced attitude that both contact with others as well as withdrawal into solitude are essential to one's well-being. The contrary is more typical: "I'm going to punish you for what you just did. Go to your room and stay there until suppertime." In this way, the child is indoctrinated with the toxic myth that being alone is synonymous with punishment and that wanting to withdraw is unhealthy.

## THE TABOO AGAINST SILENCE
The following dialogue occurred in a therapy group session after no one had spoken a word for about five minutes.

> **Aileen:** I can't stand silence. I panic. As long as somebody is talking I don't feel I have to participate. But when it's completely silent it reminds me of when I lived at home as a child. I would sit in my room wanting to be alone and yet feeling I shouldn't be enjoying the silence and the solitude. I

feel this way sometimes when I'm in a group and no one is talking—that it's up to me to say something and break the silence—as if I'm expected to do this whether I want to or not.

**Louise:** I felt so guilty because I couldn't think of anything to say during the silence. I was sitting here thinking, "Come on, think of something to say," and I couldn't. I felt sad and then all of a sudden I felt sleepy. I kept pushing myself: "Say something—come on—" and I kept thinking: "Well, what are you going to say? Some little platitude?" Then when I still didn't say anything, I felt disappointed in myself.

In our society, it is taboo for a group of people to be together in the same room without some kind of conversation continuously going on. The taboo against silence has a demand quality for many people. After two or three minutes of dead silence, most people feel a ritualistic compulsion to say something, however trite. Each person in the group is apt to feel personally responsible for doing something or saying something when the entire group is silent. To ward off the taboo against silence, some people strive to develop a repertoire of stories and jokes or to be well read and in other ways to develop a list of topics for conversation. During any period of silence they can be counted upon, to the relief of the rest of the group, to have something to say to keep the talking marathon going.

## YOU ARE NOT HELPLESS ANYMORE

Toxic myths are most obvious in their poisonous effects on the helpless child. Most of the toxic myths by which each

of us has been victimized have their origin during childhood. Because children have not yet learned to hide their
feelings behind the various façades that they will develop
through the years, we can see their pain more clearly and
perhaps then know that it is our pain also. The helplessness
of the child is real in many ways. This is, however, no
longer necessarily true as we reach adulthood. Helpless
submission to the myths, taboos and rituals each of us
experiences as toxic is no longer realistic. It is no longer
necessary to allow ourselves to be poisoned by continued
compliance because of our childhood indoctrination.

Is This
Really
What I Want
To Do
With

My Life
In This Society

## Myths About Human Behavior

Myths about human behavior keynote the life-long conflict between our natural thoughts, feeling and actions and how we are told we should (and should not) think, feel and act. Most people are needlessly tormented with confusion over what life is all about. Much of this life-long battle reflects the struggle between the relentless emerging of the self through natural growth processes and the unnecessary restrictions of toxic myths, taboos and rituals whose effects annihilate much of our humanness.

**TOXIC MYTH #29**
**To become worthwhile, decent human beings, we must denounce, and preferably eradicate, certain thoughts, feelings and impulses that exist within each of us.**

**Mother:** (*Angry at her six-year-old son who just got in a fight with his four-year-old-brother*) What on earth possessed you to push your brother down like that? He hit his forehead on the chair when he fell and it's bleeding! Do you know that you may have scarred him for life? You must be crazy to do such a terrible thing! I just don't know what got into you. You'd better watch yourself, young man, or you are going to be in a lot of trouble in this world when you get older.

Of course children do get into squabbles and sometimes even physically hurt each other. While this calls for attention, and restrictions, here the mother's approach is to make her older son feel guilty and ashamed. Discipline is a necessary component for harmonious family living; however this mother labels her son as a bad person with evil things inside of him. Such an experience for a six-year-old is traumatic in itself—seeing his younger brother's forehead bleeding. This kind of discipline lacks the love and understanding necessary (and far more effective) to raise an emotionally healthy child, even if he were the wrongdoer in a situation. This example is typical of the countless ways in which we are taught that there really are impulses within us, that we are unaware of, that might leap out at any time and alienate us from those we love and need.

The myth that we are innately dangerous creatures—socially, ethically and morally—carries into adulthood and condemns us to gnawing fears and anxieties that something dreadful might emerge from within us and surface like some horrible monster from the depths of the ocean. Once we swallow this myth, we quite logically learn to remain suspicious and distrustful of ourselves and, of course, of everyone else as well.

Toxic myths about human behavior hamper our natural ability to both regulate ourselves in our personal lives *and* cooperate with the rules and regulations necessary for group living.

**A nourishing attitude toward setting limits on behavior and creating a natural pattern of social ethics and morality focuses on the realistic consequences of a person's actions and nothing else.**

This attitude neutralizes those myths that teach us to limit our behavior by instilling guilt, shame or fear about our "animalistic" impulses. These myths ignore the fact that people are social animals and have always chosen, out of deep emotional and psychological needs, to live in groups. It is condemnation of many of our natural behavioral tendencies and the labeling of them as taboo that grossly hampers our ability to discover how to really control ourselves and how to avoid the destructive tendencies we see all around us. Ignorance, fear and distrust of ourselves make the task of blending our social and animalistic impulses unrealistically difficult. They prevent us from bringing all aspects of the vital problem of learning how to live with ourselves and others into full light, so as to examine them thoroughly and recognize that every thought, feeling and impulse is part of us. This recognition does not mean that we can necessarily act them out as we please, but it does offer the most effective approach to self-regulation *and* with the least amount of energy and effort.

## TOXIC MYTH #30
## Human beings are naturally untrustworthy.

This particular version of the myths that teach us we are inherently evil is responsible for many of society's methods of dealing with socially disruptive behavior, which, in the long run, foster *more* antisocial behavior, not less. It enhances the spare-the-rod-and-spoil-the-child approach to socially unacceptable behavior. It teaches us that the only way we will behave is through external pressure and the power to punish, which must always be close at hand. Such myths are also the basis of the lie that punishment changes behavior in the way we intend. Actually, punishment is more likely to teach us to become more clever and deceptive and to avoid getting caught. As untrustworthy creatures we must then be "broken" into submission, much as we train wild animals. This notion also fosters a paranoid attitude toward ourselves and our neighbors. The myth that we are innately untrustworthy implies that we *can* be trusted to lie, cheat, steal, kill, and so forth, and that the only thing that keeps us from doing so is constant policing by everyone. Those who believe this myth tend to interpret every act of violence as further evidence that we are indeed nothing more than animals. The exploration of other possible causes and explanations for socially destructive behavior is considered to be either irrelevant or of minor importance, or is ignored altogether.

Toxic myths about human behavior become actively manifested in our personal lives by means of the taboos and rituals that they impose on our behavior and which induce a great deal of stress and inner conflict by their unnecessary restrictions. The target area includes all the various emotional reactions and behavior patterns that do not follow the traditional *shoulds* and *should-nots* of our culture. Hence, when we break any of these taboos or fail to submit to any of these rituals, we have been taught to feel miserable, inadequate and untrustworthy. When, as happens to all of us on occasion, we do act irresponsibly, instead of seeing the incident as an example of our human imperfection, we label ourselves as totally untrustworthy.

When such experiences occur in the lives of children and they are repeatedly labeled as untrustworthy, they gradually begin to believe the myths about their innate badness. Not only does this have a destructive effect on their self-concept, but it is extremely detrimental to the sincere desires of parents and other social authorities in their task of helping children to learn to be more reliable.

Labeling children with the stamp of social disapproval does not change their behavior, it simply generates guilt and shame and teaches the child to become more clever in learning how to avoid contact and honesty with authority figures, including and especially parents. The more intensely the child struggles to escape the label of untrustworthiness and the psychic pain this produces, the more energy he will devote to discovering the methods and techniques with which to avoid being seen in this light. In this process, he simply becomes less honest and open. In no way is this likely to teach him to become more reliable or trustworthy.

## The Punishment Myth

More often than not punishment is a destructive approach to learning what is acceptable and unacceptable behavior. The prevailing attitude is that the offender is a bad person. In this respect, toxic myths teach us that if we are the kind of person we should be, we would not be punished.

The typical attitude involved in punishment ritualistically equates the act with the doer and is totally unrealistic. This has a generally toxic effect on the overall well-being and self-esteem of the offender (now victim). In essence, the whole self is condemned.

Implicit in the attitude of those who believe in punishment is the myth that, when the penalties produce enough pain or feeling of deprivation, the person will no longer want to continue the behavior for which he is being punished.

While there may be some truth to this belief, it is a fantasy that we can teach people to be loving, caring and socially responsible by punishing them sufficiently for their unacceptable behavior. The ineffectiveness of our prison system rehabilitating people is overwhelming evidence that the myth that punishment works is a lie.

The primary effects of punishment are the feelings of alienation and isolation it produces in the person being punished. This occurs initially during childhood when we are punished by a parent. The trauma is therefore more intense because we feel alienated, rejected and unloved by one or both of the two most important people in our lives—the two people on whom we are totally dependent for our very survival! This traumatic "learning process" then continues as the child is subsequently punished by authority figures outside the home.

The primary result of punishment is to teach us to think that the world is hostile and uncaring. It is in this sense the belief that punishment "works" is an extremely toxic myth, for the focal point of learning how to behave when based on punishment, then becomes a matter of learning how to protect oneself against actual or would-be punishers. This fosters "me against them" attitudes, so that when children get away with something they feel as if they have won against "them."

As punishment is primarily a process of alienation from others in which the offender is taught that he or she is unacceptable as a person, how does it happen that its use by people who love us is so prevalent? This is because punishment techniques instill powerful feelings of guilt, shame and fear that do inhibit a person's behavior, at least while under the watchful eye of some authority. The punished child may become inhibited but we delude ourselves when we equate this inhibition with learning moral, social and ethical responsibility. In addition, this only sets the stage for future explosions as the pressure from the inhibitions themselves continues to build within the child.

Often this build-up of pressure bursts through as children approach adolescence. Those who have been victimized by punishment who begin to feel their power growing are increasingly willing to test themselves by defying the punitive authorities to which they previously seemed so submissive and compliant.

**If you want to create an adult who is antisocial (as well as unhappy and emotionally unstable), punish him or her frequently and severely during childhood.**

The punishment myth is an offshoot of that constellation of false truths that teach us that human beings are essentially untrustworthy. In essence, it implies that we can be beaten into becoming worthwhile, responsible, moral human beings. In contrast, love and reward are the basic antidotes. These will teach children how to satisfy their needs and alleviate frustrations by discovering more socially acceptable attitudes and behavior patterns.

**TOXIC MYTH #31
Punishment teaches us to become responsible citizens.**

A child raised in a loving environment will respond to the setting of limits and rules of behavior when this is done in a caring and sensitive manner in which the parents are aware of how their actions affect their child. When parents are willing to provide an understandable explanation for why they don't want the child to behave in a certain way, the children will respond with much less need for specific penalties. In particular, parents should be aware that an ever-increasing amount of punishment for repeated violations strongly suggests that it is not working and, on the contrary, is becoming increasingly destructive. Most of us really sense that children learn through love; it builds their self-esteem, which leads to the development of their *own* inner desire to behave in socially acceptable ways. When this is the prevalent attitude, especially through the early years of childhood, the healthiest approach to learning with a minimal need for punishment is provided. It is therefore the most effective antidote for the poisonous effects of punishment.

Antisocial behavior is a learned pattern of reactions to the rejection or lack of love and caring (which includes neglect as well as chaotic permissiveness). Antisocial behavior is *taught* as surely as we are taught to read and write. With few exceptions of a specific nature, children who have a history of behavior problems in school and become involved in conflict with the authorities during adolescence and adulthood, invariably have a history of neglect, lack of love and understanding, or outright physical or emotional abuse.

This has created anger and frustration within them for which they have found no other resolution except to reflect the responses they have received. For example, when children are abused by parents, they learn to be abusive. When their integrity is violated and they are not listened to or understood, they in turn learn to disregard and violate the integrity of others.

Punishment always involves action *against* another person. We cling to the myth that punitive measures will stop a person from continuing to engage in unacceptable behavior. When these punitive measures don't work, the ritualistic procedure is to increase the penalty. Second offenders are treated more harshly than first offenders and so on.

More effective police action, whether parental or governmental, only deludes us into believing that the offending behavior has disappeared. Usually, it has only increased the punisher's task of perennial watchfulness. The ritualistic label for such a person is "reformed" or "rehabilitated." Yet when we take away the watchful eye of punitive authority, the same old patterns are resumed.

Despite the evidence we continue to cling to the myth that punishment will teach the offender to be a more responsible person. At best what really happens is that punishment teaches us fear and inhibition; not how to behave in a more socially acceptable manner. The offender already knows what is expected anyhow. Punishment typically teaches the offender only to be more clever, more deceptive, and in the main, motivates him to learn how not to get caught.

## Myths About Living

Most of us grow up with expectations that our lives should more or less reflect a movie version of the good life. We are taught to expect above average material success. We are taught to expect to find a vocation that will be challenging and interesting and will lead us up the ladder of success and social recognition. We are taught to expect the movie version of romantic love and marital bliss. We are taught to expect that we will achieve all these wonderful things and that we will live happily ever after. We come to believe that all these delights are not only our just due, but will be forthcoming without too much difficulty or frustration.

### TOXIC MYTH #32
### Life should be easy.

The myth that life should be easy implies that something unfair is happening when this is not the case. It becomes more evident when we have followed all the toxic demands that are supposed to be the prerequisites for the good life and we discover that it hasn't happened yet. If our life is drab, frustrating or painful, this is seen as an interlude, which we must best endure, while we await the glorious changes that we were taught would be forthcoming. False hopes are created that the future will be better and easier because that's the way it's supposed to be.

> Dottie's thirtieth birthday was nothing short of traumatic. It came as a sudden shock to her that "here I am at the end of my youth still working a nine-to-five clerical job and sharing an apartment with a girlfriend." The more she evaluated her life, the more depressed she became. She had a brief marriage when she was nineteen, but her husband, who had planned to become a dentist, dropped out of school six months later and took a job in a paint store. Till then she had dreams of working to support him through school, after which he would become a successful dentist and they would raise a beautiful family in a beautiful home in the suburbs with all the trimmings that she felt would be forthcoming.

> Her husband had done his best to get good grades, but the competition for the limited number of openings in dental schools was too intense. His grades were above average, but not good enough. A friend who had gone to work directly from high school offered him a job in a paint store. The thought of earning a weekly salary with which he could buy the things they both wanted seemed to compensate for his frustration. But instead, he began staying away nights and coming home drunk. When Dottie also

discovered he was spending his evenings with a young divorcé he met at work, she moved back to her parent's home and got a divorce. During her twenties, she had several serious relationships which all ended with more disappointment for her.

With her thirtieth birthday she felt bewildered. Somehow she had missed the boat and was way off schedule in what she had expected out of life. She saw very little future for herself in her drab and intolerable life. Trying to grab some of the good things of life, she used her credit to purchase a sports car, a trip to Europe and other things she knew at the time she couldn't afford and which did not fill up the emptiness she felt. At 32 she was deeply in debt, lonely, disillusioned and made her first suicide attempt. After Dottie began therapy following her attempted suicide, she proclaimed, "Life is just too damn hard. Nobody ever told me it would be like this." Raised with the traditional myths about the role of a woman, she had believed that a Prince Charming would come along and provide her with all the lovely things that had been portrayed to her as being part of the good life. It just wasn't supposed to be this hard.

Myths that provide a feeling of optimism and motivate us to strive for what we want are nourishing as long as they do not suggest unrealistic expectations. Myths are toxic if they indoctrinate us with false promises, such as the promise that, if we follow the rituals and obey the taboos, our lives will one day somehow be suddenly altered for the better.

When we are indoctrinated with the lie that life should be easy, our discovery of what living is really like becomes an unnecessarily hard reality to accept because of our expectation that it is supposed to be easy. Most people tend to cling to the myth insisting that somehow there's got to be an easier way, that they just haven't found it yet. Or the big break hasn't occurred and they continue to wait and hope instead of either changing their expectations or their actions. Meanwhile, the appreciation of much that could be meaningful in their existing life is ignored because they are future-oriented toward the goals and expectations they have always been led to believe would be theirs.

Another poisonous effect of this attitude is that it stifles our motivation to initiate efforts on our own behalf and to really struggle for what we want. After all, while parents may tell us that life is a struggle, these are usually empty words lost in the shadow of the glorious myth that life is easy and happiness is our birthright and will be delivered to us simply on that basis.

## TOXIC MYTH #33
### Pain and suffering should not be a part of life.

The fairytale version of what life should be like also includes the myth that pain and suffering do not occur except for specific, unfortunate tragedies that befall us through bad luck. A very prevalent attitude among adults is the feeling that they have had more than their share of pain, suffering and misfortune, that these are things that happen to others but not to them. Myths that paint a rosy picture of life further enhance the idea that, when we are unhappy or frustrated, it means something has gone wrong with the game-plan of life.

**TOXIC MYTH #34**
**We are special.**

This myth further perpetuates the fairytale that one day things will stop going wrong and we will live happily ever after. It teaches us that, because we are special, happy experiences are to be expected while tragedies should not happen to us, particularly because we have done nothing to bring them on. The we-are-special myth separates us from the rest of nature and implies that what happens to all other living creatures should not happen to us. It teaches that we are a unique species with special privileges that somehow supersede the laws of nature. We are led to believe that the misfortunes and tragedies that some people experience reflect evil influences in the world and these are not supposed to exist in the first place.

Specialness myths have a twofold toxic effect. First, although the potentials of human experiences are practically unlimited, they encourage us to believe we are something more than our actual experience tells us we are. Second, we cling to our expectations and rights, which we honestly believe we have coming to us, and *wait* for "nice" things to happen and "bad" things to stop happening. This only enhances feelings of helplessness and inadequacy when happiness is not forthcoming. The likely conclusion is that we must be doing something wrong, particularly when we feel that we have had more than our share of misfortune, disappointments and tragedies.

**What's In a Name?**

Gladys and Marie had been close friends for many years. Both were executive secretaries, and they often imagined how much fun it would be to work for the same company. When Gladys learned that one of the other secretaries in her office was leaving, she put in a word with her boss and Marie got the job. To prepare Marie for her new position, Gladys described each of their fellow employees to her:

**Gladys:** Let me tell you what some of the bosses and some of the other people here are like so you'll know how to handle them.

**Marie:** That's neat. I'll have everyone pegged before I even start to work. Let's begin with my boss. What's he like?

**Gladys:** Well, Mr. Larson is a real family man. He keeps pictures of his wife and kids on the desk and has new pictures of them each year. That means he's straight. Don't fool around or flirt with him and it's better to give him the impression that you date very little. Also, watch your language around him: he doesn't like hip talk.

**Marie:** I get the message. Mr. Larson is uptight, so I should behave like a prim and proper young lady—like I was his daughter (*both laugh*).

**Gladys:** Now the one to really watch out for is Mr. Bradford. He's an ex-Army colonel and you know what that means. If he sees you slipping out early, he'll send a note over to your boss. You know how Army colonels are. You have to behave according to the rule book. Whenever anybody informs on someone else about goofing off or being late, we always know it's Bradford. He always looks the same with that stern face, erect posture and shoulders back. He never smiles, but what can you expect from an Army colonel.

Another one to watch out for is Mrs. Young. She's the assistant office manager. She was hospitalized for a mental illness several years ago. So no matter what you do, always humor her and never get her upset or anything because if she gets irritated, she might become irrational. Give her a wide berth and a lot of lip service.

Then there's Jonesey, as we call Mr. Jones behind his back. He's the best boss. Everybody knows that he was a playboy and that his millionaire father practically forced the company to hire him as an executive. Now he's kind of settled down. But a playboy is a playboy, so you don't have to take him too seriously.

This dialogue illustrates the ritualistic tendency, if not outright compulsion, to label persons and sort their behavior into neat compartments. (This is also known as psyching people out.) Doing so provides us with a feeling of security about those who are unfamiliar and therefore threatening. Once we have labeled them, we can attribute to them the well-established stereotypes we have been taught to associate with that label and those who wear it (e.g., patriotic, evil, un-American, atheist, millionaire). Labeling human beings and categorizing their behavior according to their label is a procedure that distorts reality and perpetuates toxic myths.

## TOXIC MYTH #35
**Labeling someone increases our understanding of what that person is like.**

The either-or attitude is the most common form of labeling and reflects delusive thinking. It ignores the human being as a dynamic process comprising some of *all* the qualities subsumed under the countless labels humankind has arbitrarily invented. It distorts reality by forcing people and their attitudes, beliefs and behavior into one of two possible categories. This black-or-white categorizing sets the stage for judging ourselves and others as okay–not okay, good–bad, right–wrong, friend–enemy. The labeling myth is toxic in that it leads us to believe that categorizing increases our understanding of other people and tells us the best way to relate to them — or to manipulate them.

Peggy and Les have been married for six years. In the last year their relationship has deteriorated markedly and is now characterized by frequent bickering. They never see anything the same way, and during their quarrels each tries to establish himself or herself as right and the other as wrong. Because he had not been feeling well, Les went to his doctor for a complete physical. The following dialogue occurred the evening Les came home with the results of this examination.

> **Les:** The doctor said that there is really nothing wrong with me, but he sees clear signs of hypertension and my blood pressure is a little high. He asked if I had any problems. I told him that you and I have been having marital problems. He suggested we see a psychologist for marriage counseling.

**Peggy:**  I knew it! You're the neurotic in this family, not me. You're the one who's always irritable and grouchy.

**Les:**  Damn, you make me angry! I think if I got rid of you, I might get rid of my hypertension at the same time!

**Peggy:**  That's it. Blame me for everything! You just never want to accept that you're wrong. You're the one that's got the symptoms. You're the one that's got the hypertension. I'm telling you, you're the neurotic and you want to put it on me again, like you always do. That's what you neurotics do anyway, that's part of your neurosis. You go see a shrink and get yourself fixed up and rid of your neurosis. I'm the normal one around here. I can get along with anybody.

This dialogue is a typical example of the reality distortion labeling encourages in our thinking. Peggy insists she is the "normal" one. The assumption is that, because they are having so much difficulty, Les deserves the label "neurotic." Peggy justifies labeling her husband as "the neurotic one" because he shows symptoms of stress. As is usually true of such labeling, the effect is purely destructive and, in this example, detrimental to their marriage. The one labeled "bad" always gets back at the other, one way or another. In the long run they both lose because such games only contribute to the deterioration of their relationship.

Labeling does relieve anxiety. Giving something or someone a descriptive name does at least remove it from the dreaded area of the unknown. When we are unable to understand or cope with problems, we often react as if a magical transformation has occurred when the problem is given a name or label. We can then respond ritualistically to all the qualities associated with that particular label. When we do so, however, we cease to question what the problem *really* involves, and can no longer make effective efforts to solve it.

All behavior is a matter of degree. Any kind of human behavior we might describe varies in intensity and frequency, as well as in numerous other ways. When we label or categorize human behavior, what we usually are referring to is some extreme form of that behavior, for it is only in the extreme that we have a clear picture of what the label means.

Once this labeling begins, an insidious cause-and-effect pattern perpetuates it indefinitely. We accept a particular label and then act as if we are indeed the kind of person described by that label. When situations elicit from us the behavior attributed to that kind of person, we use this fact to verify our fears that we do indeed deserve the label. Any person of normal intelligence can accumulate some evidence to justify any label. The falseness of such an approach becomes apparent when we are made aware that the data that would contradict the label are invariably ignored and information is excluded for some reason or explained away.

Any predetermined label has a toxic effect on all future relationships. As we become aware that all reality is a matter of degree, we can break out of the compartmentalized existence we create by labeling and allowing ourselves to be labeled. The most effective antidote to this is to approach each new encounter with an open mind and allow the subsequent interactions to develop their own identity.

## Sacred Cows: Myths About Heroes and Experts

All toxic myths either distort reality or reflect obsolete attitudes and beliefs. Most of the myths discussed in this book have so little connection with reality they can be termed irrational, yet they are accepted uncritically by vast numbers of people. Although these people know the myths are without substance, their emotional attitudes cause them to react as if they are valid.

**TOXIC MYTH #36**
**If a person is successful in one field of**
**human endeavor, he or she is an expert in**
**all things.**

Ours is a society of experts. We have experts in every field of human endeavor. While being an expert is not toxic in itself, the attitude we adopt toward experts and the power with which we endow them may be. Toxic myths foster a ritualistic attitude bordering on reverence toward experts, even when they generalize their expertise far beyond their particular field of accomplishment to include areas in which they are totally ignorant or in which their opinion is irrelevant. When such experts speak out on issues about which they have no knowledge or experience other than their personal opinion, or when they state their preferences for various styles or products, people act as if the experts' opinions and preferences are somehow more valid than their own, even when it is simply a matter of personal taste.

In our society, physical beauty, success in the entertainment industry, or possession of great wealth may qualify a person as an "expert." Celebrities are paid to endorse all kinds of commodities, movements, and even other persons, although they may know little about what they are endorsing. The athlete who returns from the Olympics with a string of gold medals is an automatic millionaire because advertising agencies and manufacturers know that his or her endorsement (having nothing to do with their extraordinary neuromuscular development or athletic skills) will sell their shirts, cereals, perfumes or cars. Because of their fame, wealth or beauty, we assume these "experts" have leadership potential. We endow wealthy industrialists, whose main claims to fame may be the fact that their grandfathers happened to buy land that 50 years later turned out to be oil fields. We give away our power by endowing them with wisdom and seeking their advice on all kinds of matters, including social and political issues. We may even elect them to public office largely on the basis of the notoriety their wealth, success or appealing appearance can obtain.

Our ritualistic admiration of celebrities and other experts is testimony to the ability of toxic myths to render us stupid. In India, so-called sacred cows are considered holy, are protected from harm, and in essence can do no wrong. A somewhat similar attitude applies to the ritualistic manner in which we behave toward various categories of heroes and experts within our own culture. We relate to our "sacred cows" as if they possess attributes that make them superior to us as *human beings*. Such a ritualistic attitude is toxic when it causes us to react to our "experts" as if they are superior in any areas other than the ones in which they have demonstrated their skill, experience or expertise.

## SOMEBODY KNOWS BETTER THAN ME

Sacred cow attitudes stem from the myth that other people are more capable of deciding what is best for us than we are ourselves. Such an assumption may be valid in specific areas of knowledge and experience, such as medicine or auto mechanics but is toxic when applied to our individual selves and our personal tastes, preferences, attitudes and beliefs. In certain areas this idea that "I know better than you, so listen to me" borders on the ridiculous—for example, a television commercial in which a movie star recommends that we use the laxative he or she uses. Yet we choose to be victims of these toxic myths and we *do* listen. We *are* influenced by outstanding scientists' endorsements of candidates for public office, as if their scientific contributions render their opinions of politics, social issues and political candidates more valid than our own. Similarly, we make other celebrities, who are often simply physically attractive men and women, into quality experts. We listen to them when we choose our breakfast cereals, skin creams, shaving lotions and endless other commodities.

**Because it is taboo in our culture to feel confused, uncertain or unpopular, WE ALLOW others who have won some kind of popularity contest to tell us what our preferences should be rather than take the risk of deciding this for ourselves.**

Heroes and experts flourish in our society because of our taboos against suspecting them of being no less corrupt, dishonest, immoral, or self-centered than the rest of us. Our mythology teaches us that they are virtuous "good people" unless clearly proven otherwise. When they are discovered and exposed as corrupt and dishonest, it is a newsworthy event typically referred to as a "scandal." Such scandals would be much less newsworthy were we not initially the victims of ritualistic expectations regarding those who gain fame and notoriety.

## Myths About the Medical World

**Vera:** (*During a group psychotherapy session*) My doctor told me that I had to have surgery. I was upset and wanted to talk about it but he said he had other patients waiting. I wanted to know what I was supposed to do. I've never had surgery and nobody would give me any answers or tell me what to expect. I'm not a doctor. I even felt guilty, because he said he was so busy. I feel like I'm not important enough to take up his time.

So I made a special consultation appointment and he told me: "Your surgery is very minor. It's also not as uncommon as you think it is." I got angry and said: "It isn't minor to me. It might be minor to you, but it's really important to me. You treat me like I'm a child. If you tell me it's nothing, I should just believe it's nothing. If you say it's very light, I should act like it's very light."

Then he said: "You're getting hysterical. You're making too much out of it. I see you're upset and I have a lot of patients waiting. I'm all booked up. Have your family physician call me."

Then I got angry and told him: "You keep putting me off. You never have time and I feel the bind. I need you and I trust your medical judgment. I don't want to argue. I need you and yet I'm so angry with you I'm afraid you won't help me.

His reply was: "You're just being neurotic. What you need is a psychiatrist."

**Joan:** I find I get into the same trap you're in because I tend to think of doctors as so powerful. They know what they're doing and I should listen to them. But I'm paying them and I have a right to ask for what I want to know about my own medical problems.

**Mary:** (*Who happens to be a Registered Nurse*) Everybody kneels down. Have you ever heard nurses talk about doctors like it's a privilege to kneel at their feet?

**Margaret:** I had an experience I'll share. This doctor I was seeing misdiagnosed me and recommended an immediate hysterectomy. I consulted two other doctors who agreed with each other and disagreed with him. My insurance only covered parts of the visits. I only paid him what the insurance paid and wrote him a letter explaining why. I received no response. Two weeks later he turned the bill over to a collection agency.

The rituals and taboos with which we relate to medical doctors make them sacred cows in our society. It is taboo to relate to physicians primarily as highly trained technicians whose skills are often life-saving. (*Toxic ritual has it that, traditionally, the physician should be male.*) It is taboo for us to accept the reality that doctors' services, invaluable as they may be, are largely unrelated to their human qualities, their caringness, their honesty or their genuine concern (or lack of it) for their patients.

## TOXIC MYTH #37
**Professional people in general are dedicated. They choose to practice their profession primarily for altruistic reasons rather than for social status or economic rewards.**

Many professional people, of course, do treat their clients as human beings, are interested in them and do respect their integrity. They are direct in discussing problems and solutions in language that is easily understood. Others reinforce the traditional mythical attitudes of their profession and act as if they were ordained. They decide whether or not the client should be told the truth. Some even consider it taboo for a client to question their decisions. In general, toxic myths about professional people perpetuate the stereotype of an unselfish, always available, dedicated human being. We continue to expect a personal concern and an intimate relationship, which is obsolete. We continue to expect physicians to relate to us as they have been traditionally portrayed. We see them as modern versions of the horse-and-buggy doctors of 50 years ago—even why they may see 50 or 100 patients a day—or expect the attorney to provide free services in defense of the innocent.

For most people, hospitals are also sacred cows in institutional form. The average patient entering a hospital surrenders his or her integrity the moment he or she is admitted. Ritual demands, passive compliance and unquestioning submission. Even when the person admitted is acutely ill, he or she is often required to fill out a questionnaire and establish credit before receiving treatment. Patients must submit passively to ritualistic hospital procedure: "Wake up, it's time for our bath, sleeping pill, etc." This is the ritual and you will obey! Protest is taboo and will probably merely result in resentment by the staff and the label "difficult patient."

The typical modern hospital is a factory, mass-producing services for customers for a profit. Its routines and efficiency-oriented procedures may well be the most effective way of treating large numbers of ill people. It is our responsibility when we cling to toxic myths about hospitals and continue to expect physicians to fit an image. We stereotype them with the obsolete attitudes and mythical qualities of the "experts" who, because of their particular specialty, should also fill our needs for mother-figure, father-confessor, and friend who cares for us personally and even intimately.

Our culture clings to unique patterns of myths, rituals and taboos toward a vast range of successful achievers: scientists, judges, lawyers, psychologists, the clergy, generals and admirals, as well as athletes, millionaires and all kinds of celebrities. These categories of expertise are, of course, composed of people no different from the rest of us. The experts discussed in this chapter illustrate the toxic effects that such myths, rituals and taboos have on most of us.

The obvious antidote to the toxic myths about experts requires, first, that we be aware of their fallibility, especially when we are relating to them as authorities in any area other than where they have the credentials that qualify them as experts in their field. Second, when we seek their expertise, we need to be aware that they are in no way superior to the rest of us as human beings. In reality, an expert is nothing more than a person who has some specific skill, knowledge or talent and is not necessarily outstanding beyond that category. Last, we need to respect our own decision after we have listened to the experts. In the final analysis, we must rely on our trust that a particular expert knows what he or she is doing. This in no way precludes the need for communication and dialogue between ourselves and the experts, nor does it exonerate us from responsibility for having accepted an expert's advice.

## Myths About Death and Dying

### THE DENIAL OF DEATH

Toxic myths proliferate in the fertile fields of ignorance. Because no one has experienced death and returned to tell us about it, taboos, rituals and myths about death are rampant. Largely, death has been the domain of religions since the beginning of history, and the taboos and rituals reflect the teachings of each specific religion. In our society, the subject of death itself is taboo, and we observe many rituals to avoid awareness of the obvious fact that every living thing dies. Until very recently, the subject of death was barely discussed at all. The word itself was taboo.

Denying the physical death of the body is a prevailing ritual. Funeral homes do everything possible to make a corpse look "alive" because there are strict taboos against seeing a body in its natural state of death. Even hospitals, police and the military ritualistically cover the body, and especially the face, of someone who has just died. The very color of death is forbidden to our sight: regardless of how grotesque the cosmetics may be, it is essential that the skin coloring of the corpse be hidden. In hospitals, such terms as "expired" or "deceased" are used when a patient dies. Mortuaries have "slumber rooms," and corpses buried in the ground are "put to rest." Confronted with these taboos and rituals, each individual finds it unnecessarily difficult to come to terms with the inevitability of his or her own death.

Such myths, with their dishonesty, denials of reality, and anxiety-producing qualities hamper our ability to live the full and meaningful lives we are capable of living. These myths create a phobic attitude about death so intense that death becomes a major obsession throughout the lives of countless numbers of people.

## TOXIC MYTH #38
## Death is something to be feared.

Healthy people want to live. We seek aliveness in ourselves and others. We are attracted to what is exciting, stimulating and life-giving. We don't want to die and we don't want those we love to die. The sadness and mourning we experience about death can be considered a natural reaction reflecting the laws of self-preservation. We want to stay alive and we want those who add meaning and aliveness to our existences to remain alive also. While we feel the sadness of the loss that death brings when someone we love dies, the dread of death is enormously, and unnecessarily enhanced by toxic myths, taboos and rituals about the death process.

Toxic myths about death are quite another matter. They focus primarily on what it means to be dead. They tell us about death as if it were something we will experience: "One day I shall die and then I'll find out what it really is like to be dead."

**Myths about death are toxic when they are intended to scare the life out of us.**

Myths about death are toxic when they instill in us fears about death that go beyond our natural desire to stay

alive. Such myths frequently use our fear of death to manipulate us into various patterns of conformity. Death is the
most obvious, although not necessarily the most feared,
ultimate form of punishment, and toxic myths about death
carry the theme of eternal suffering, punishment and
damnation. Thus, the thought of death brings with it the
awesome fear of endless suffering.

When we have not been poisoned excessively by toxic
myths about death, we are capable of coming to terms
with the inevitability of our death as we live our lives. This
natural process is more than the poetic notion that there is
"a time to die." However unwanted, the end of life need
not evoke the kind of dread that destroys our ability to
live fully *and* joyfully.

The antidote to our anxieties and fears about death and
dying begins with our willingness to face the fact of death
and in this way becoming more aware that we have choices
about how we look at death and how we define its meaning. This means letting go of the obvious: that, psychologi-
cally speaking, death *is* part of everyone's life.

**Avoiding the issue of death makes death
more frightening and prevents us from
fully living our lives.**

How we want to die is another issue about which important
choices are possible. Traditionally, our toxic mythology
about death dictated a strict taboo against taking any such
options. Someone else (e.g., a member of the family or a
physician) ritualistically decides whether or not a patient
should even be told he or she was dying. Traditionally,
the decision, with the best of intentions, was that it was
better *not* to know. Those closest to the patient were then
forced to go through the grotesque rituals of denial and

avoidance. Some of us may indeed prefer not to know, and this preference is perfectly valid; but this practice cheats others of the right to come to terms with death. It prevents them from saying their good-byes and does not allow all concerned to prepare themselves, as much as possible, for the event of death.

The challenges to the toxic myths, taboos and rituals about death and dying have only very recently begun. It is an area in which a great deal more human understanding is certainly long overdue. It is surely possible that many more of us can find our personal ways to come to terms with death and thereby free ourselves from its toxic effects on our lives.

Is This
Really
What I Want
To Do
With

My Working Life

# The Myth of Normalcy

**TOXIC MYTH #39**
**The normal person should be a lifelong**
**achiever who continues to strive**
**for more and more success, not for the**
**gratifications of work, but to accumulate**
**material possessions, wealth, social status**
**and power.**

Ignorance is the most fertile breeding ground for toxic myths, taboos and rituals. Our ignorance (ignoring our existing knowledge) about what a normal human being is really like, can scarcely be overestimated. It is not surprising that toxic myths about the "well-adjusted," "normal" person are rampant. According to these myths, we expect ourselves to be cheerful, outgoing and happy most of the time—especially when others are present—whether we feel like it or not. For many people it is socially risky to appear down, irritated or tired. There is a taboo against settling for being average in performance and accomplishments. The normalcy myth teaches us that, if we are only average, we are, socially speaking, failures.

## FITS AND MISFITS

The poisonous effect of the normalcy myth is inherent in its ritualistic attitude that, when we do not conform, we are social misfits. All conformity myths consider the individual to be less important than the standards expected by the group, and those who do not comply (or appear not to comply) are seen as deserving of social isolation or other retributions. Indeed, there is rarely a shortage of self-righteous people who see it as their duty to carry out this kind of punishment. They attack the "offender's" self-esteem as a person and often leave him or her feeling permanently branded as a misfit. This destructive cycle is further reinforced by the common fantasy of most people who feel they are misfits and that everyone else "fits" willingly, even joyfully, into compliance with the taboos and rituals toxic myths demand.

Carol, Dick and Larry were born into a family where ambition and outstanding achievement were the highest virtues. As far back as each could remember, their father, in particular, had urged them to be ambitious, to stand out above the crowd. To be a continuously outstanding achiever was the only acceptable behavior. The older children carried this philosophy into adulthood. Carol became a successful trial attorney and Dick, a vice-president in a good-sized corporation.

Larry was actually more intellectually gifted than his older siblings. Yet, somehow, despite all the preaching of his parents, the idea of just being ambitious as a value in and of itself simply did not appeal to him. In high school Larry showed unusual artistic ability and won several scholarships. By the time he was 25, he was well on his way to becoming a successful artist.

Larry's attitude infuriated his father, because he knew Larry was clearly the most talented and the brightest of his three children. He resisted Larry's interest in art, telling him: "Art is something you do as a hobby. Nobody expects to make a living being an artist these days. After you are a success, you can turn to that kind of recreation if you want to." For Larry's father, ambition and achievement were not only the prime virtues but they had to find expression in certain traditional areas, and art was not one of these. Nevertheless, through his high school and college years, the public recognition Larry received even began to sway his father. Maybe art had something worthwhile for a person after all!

When Larry was about 30, he was already a successful portrait painter whose income equaled that of either of his brother and sister. His father now really appreciated him because of the monetary value of his work.

One day Larry announced that he was giving up doing portraits to go live in Europe and study other art media. His father was not only perplexed but furious: "How can you throw away a successful career with a bright future in a field where you are already established just to go off in search of some newfangled ideas. Where is your practicality, boy?"

Nevertheless, Larry proceeded with his plans. He closed his studio and left for Europe. With great reluctance, his father concluded that Larry was simply the black sheep of the family and that at least he could be grateful that his other two children had enough common sense to see what's important in this world.

The more powerful the social-fitting game, the greater its destructive effects on the individual and eventually on society as a whole. Individual uniqueness and open expression are necessary to encourage the creative potential every society needs if it is to adapt itself to changing reality and its evolving needs. Destroying what is obsolete is an essential part of the creative growth process within each society, as it is within each person. Rules and regulations can hopelessly stifle this creative process. The normalcy myth can make us feel too threatened to dare to challenge its demands for compliance to countless rituals and taboos. In contrast, the normalcy myth tells us that sheeplike, herd conformity is more valuable and that we should avoid thinking, feeling and, most of all, expressing anything new or different.

**The normalcy myth places the highest
value on winning the popularity contest.**

Popularity contests come in countless variations. Each of them promises that, if we excel and are "winners" in some field of human endeavor, this achievement will bring with it all those rewards and gratifications that will provide us with a happy and meaningful life. Those who fail to accomplish some outstanding achievement are taught that the consequence is a life of mediocrity and endless frustration, which is their just do because they have failed to achieve "winner" status.

Because relatively few of us can be "winners" in the sense of excelling over everyone else, the most obvious destructive effects of this myth are the feelings of inadequacy, aloneness and alienation from society generated in the "losers." The myth deprives many of us of group acceptance, an essential psychological ingredient necessary in developing our sense of human dignity. In a nourishing atmosphere, this feeling of acceptance develops from doing things that are experimentally meaningful and gratifying in themselves, not from evaluation of our accomplishments by comparative measures to determine whether he or she is a worthwhile human being.

## YOU SHOULD CHANGE

The "change yourself" rituals admonish us that, when we feel frustrated or unhappy within our existence, it is because we are unacceptable and inadequate as we are and that our only hope is to become different. This offshoot of the normalcy myth implies that there is something wrong with us, that we are defective and need fixing.

> **Mary:** I'll never change, I'm always going to be the same. If only I could get my head on straight, then I'd be okay. I've gotta be different from what I've been all my life.
>
> **Alice:** Yeah, my folks always told me I'd better change my ways or I'd be sorry later.
>
> **Jim:** In the movies somehow the shrink fixes the patient and the patient lives happily ever after—or jumps off a cliff. Either they make it, or that's the end of them and something drastic has to happen. They just aren't going to be able to get what they want in the world *as they are!*
>
> **Mary:** The part about changing really bothers me, too. Part of my evaluation of myself is that I need to change—or else.
>
> **Bob:** I've stopped lecturing myself and quit busting my ass trying to be different. There is no way to try to grow. I like myself better when I stop trying and start trusting myself. If I pay attention to me and what

I need, I learn more about who I am. I don't mean in my work situation where I know I have to please my boss. I get paid for my performance and if I don't shape up I'll get fired. That's okay, even if I don't like it. But I no longer feel I have to do that in my personal life. If my girlfriend doesn't see me as an okay guy, I think I can find someone else who does. If I want to make more money, I'll do it because I want to, not because she says I'm weak if I don't.

Jim: Right on. If a cop stops me and he's got it in his mind to write me a ticket, he's going to write it. I might stand on my head and he'll still write it. I can't dictate to the whole world.

Mary: That's what all this means to me. I never will do everything that other people expect of me and I can't make them get off my back. It's all up to me and the way I handle things. I don't have to be a different person. When I handle my problems more to my liking I feel that I'm growing.

Jim: Sure, that's the way. That's how I really find my own power and become more effective. What am I going to do if I'm frustrated by a situation or a relationship? What is my decision? What is the best I can do? If I know this, I'm in charge of me. If I start protesting what the other person is doing and it gets to an I-gotta-change-them, they-gotta-change-me situation, I just make myself uptight, and it never seems to work anyhow.

In this dialogue, Mary shows herself to be a victim of the normalcy myth. As she struggles to meet the expectations of those around her, she is trapped in her own conviction that their approval of her performance is the only basis on which she can feel good about herself. Bob and Jim are focused on the realistic limits of this struggle: that sometimes we must meet the expectations of others. But, as Jim points out, when it comes to his intimate life, he takes the opposite stand from that which the normalcy myth demands and he centers on himself and follows the flow of his own needs. Being centered on himself in this way means that he lives his life as he sees fit and with a sense of his own approval of himself as a worthwhile, loving human being. Of course, he also wants others to appreciate or approve of him, but this approval from others remains of secondary importance.

A nourishing society encourages values reflecting a wide variety of human needs and potentials. It recognizes the value of varying attitudes and behavior patterns and allows for the vast scope of individual differences exhibited in the needs, abilities and talents within any society. The normalcy myth would have us all strive toward a much more limited range of acceptable goals involving a more narrow concept of "normal" values and attitudes, making real individuality taboo.

## The Popularity Contest

### THE SUCCESS, COMPETITION AND ACHIEVEMENT MYTHS

Success myths are based on the notion that we must meet certain criteria to be deemed worthwhile. They imply that we are incompetent, or at least second-rate, until we have succeeded in jumping a series of hurdles: only then have we won the right to feel we are really acceptable. These myths are toxic because, at best, they bestow rewards on a few and ignore the emotional pain and the feelings of failure and inadequacy that are the lot of the vast majority of "ordinary" people.

Success, competition and achievement myths tell us that life is an endless series of races. There is always someone to beat, and there is always someone trying to beat us. We are encouraged to be competitive, as if competing and winning are automatically virtuous. In so doing, we ignore the isolation and alienation that result from competition. On the one hand, we need intimacy and love; on the other, we learn so early that being lovable means being successful (and vice-versa) and that one of the best ways, if not the very best way, to be successful is by excelling over or defeating others. The competition myth says that a person is more lovable when he or she "wins" economically, socially or otherwise.

Yet, these same attitudes, which we are taught are so desirable in the "outside world," are taboo within our families. This initial division of "us" against "them" begins the alienating process that unfolds in other areas of living and creates within us an attitude that "outsiders" are our enemies. The competition and achievement myths teach us *not* to feel our kinship with all humankind. Beginning with our family against the world, it becomes our neighborhood against others, our school against others, our country against others, even our "God" against others. Little wonder that paranoia, not as a psychiatric diagnosis but as a personality pattern, is rampant within individuals in our society.

Last, the competition ritual reinforces the myth that a mature person doesn't need anyone, that mature adults handle their needs without help from anyone. In our culture, millions of men and women are obsessed with the idea of being "strong." For them, asking for help from others is taboo. (Success myths have traditionally eliminated women because, in the past, it was taboo for them to compete, especially against men. As we move toward greater equality for women, they too are increasingly drawn into the rituals of the competition-success-achievement rat race.) Dependency needs become taboo and are denied or suppressed. And then we wonder why so many people feel alone and alienated from each other.

It is because they have swallowed the myth that survival means an endless battle against others, and competition is ritualistically substituted for cooperation: "If I'm as good as I should be, I should be able to do it without help." Such men and women are often proud of their ability to hide their needs for dependency and emotional nourishment from others and to make themselves appear totally independent. Their "strength" usually gains for them the admiration and respect of others because of it. They seem to be in an enviable position, yet, lurking within them, usually with some awareness, are the same hidden fears and anxieties that exist within the rest of us.

Often, for example, such men and women are obsessed with fears of suffering financial reverses, becoming chronically ill or physically handicapped. There is always a part within them, from which they cannot escape, that tells them the obvious: as human beings they are not omnipotent; no one is free from the possible calamities of life, and any of us can suddenly find ourselves very much dependent on others.

When we are willing to face this obvious fact about life, we set the stage for developing our potentials so that we do indeed become more and more capable. We then live our lives with greater self-reliance and keener awareness of our many existing needs that must be filled by others. We no longer struggle against ourselves or try to shove down our own throats a mythical list of what we should and should not feel or need.

## I'M NOT AS DUMB AS I USED TO BE

(*George was relating his own story.*) I was 33 years old when I woke up. Until then my life was a series of automatic responses to what others told me I should do. I executed these demands diligently without questioning whether or not they were what I wanted. Questioning was forbidden anyhow. I grew up under a fixed set of rules and regulations of what I should do and shouldn't do and I always responded appropriately. I was a good boy. Regardless of how I felt, I complied with the demands of my parents and the adult world, endlessly struggling to meet their expectations or get their approval.

Within myself I always looked to some future time when I would achieve some level of acceptance after which I would be free to be me. I was interested in pleasing everyone but myself. My hope was always that by pleasing them I would in turn get what I wanted from them. This never happened. When I wanted to seek satisfaction or pleasure for myself, I invariably went about it with as much secrecy as possible.

Regardless of what I wanted to do, I was always apprehensive that I would be discovered and challenged. Whenever I was caught—and it happened often—I felt embarrassed, and ashamed. I was taught that joy and pleasure were of no value. The important thing was to work, excel and climb the

ladder of success in the material and social world . . .
and to rest in between so I could continue these
pursuits relentlessly. A person was good in terms of
how many friends he had and how much money and
possessions he had been able to accumulate. I did it
and it was empty. There wasn't any prize after all.
I was 33, a millionaire, a pillar of the community.
I also had high blood pressure and was 50 pounds
overweight. That's when I started to wake up.

George's statement typifies the attitude of those victimized
by the competition-achievement-success myth. No one
had ever promised George in so many words that, after he
reached certain goals, he would be more loved and his
needs would be responded to more fully. Rather, like most
of us, George made this assumption when, as a child, he
did not feel loved and accepted. Like most of us when we
are confused and frustrated, George searched for some
explanation for his feelings of being unloved: "Why am I
unlovable? What did I do wrong?"

It is under these circumstances that toxic myths really
take their toll. For all around him, from numerous sources
there have always been the countless versions of the hero
and the heroine, the victor, the great achiever who wins
everyone's love and admiration with his or her accomplishments. Feeling lost and bewildered about what is
wrong when we feel unloved, most of us conclude that we
need to demonstrate that we are lovable. This kind of
thinking is poisonous because it causes us to look toward
the outside world as the primary source of our accep-
tability and lovableness. We believe we must be outstanding—or we are failures. We then remain at the mercy of all
the whims, idiocyncrasies and neurotic patterns of those
around us.

George woke up at 33 to the realization that winning the popularity contest was not bringing him what he wanted. In his own words, "I wised up and decided that I was going to do the things that pleased me or made me feel good and that maybe—just maybe—other people might love and appreciate me anyhow."

## ANYONE CAN BE PRESIDENT
In the center of American mythology is another obsolete idea: through ambition, diligence and hard work, any individual can rise to unlimited heights no matter how lowly his or her beginning. Horatio Alger stories and other such fairy tales about people who find success delude us into believing that success will bring love, happiness and control over our lives and the lives of others. "Success story" myths encourage us to compete with each other in a rat race, which by definition means that the vast majority must lose. Yet we are taught that anyone can be successful, that there is nothing stopping us from reaching the top. Most people caught in this ritualistic game of winning the popularity contest experience it as an endless battle filled mostly with despair and frustration, yet they continue to dedicate their time and energy to the struggle to be winners. Some, of course, do succeed. For most of us success stories are something we read, dream about and envy or resent in those who seem to have "made it." Believing in them is a popular way of poisoning ourselves and wasting our lives while we wait and hope.

## HEROES ARE MORE LOVABLE
All cultures extol the virtues of their heroes and heroines whose accomplishments reflect their values. Hero-worship has a toxic effect when we believe we must be outstanding—or we are failures. Every boy should want to be a champion athlete and every girl a Miss America. If we don't

want this, the success myth implies that there is something lacking.

Achievement myths are toxic because at best, they bestow rewards on a few and ignore the emotional pain and the feelings of failure and inadequacy that are the lot of the vast majority of "ordinary" people.

## Performance Myths

### YOU SHOULD TRY HARDER

Performance myths indoctrinate us with the toxic attitude that the real significance of what we do depends on the end product of our efforts. Performance myths hold us on trial, often throughout our entire lives. We are always measuring ourselves, or subject to being measured, on the basis of our accomplishments or the lack of them.

Excellence is not toxic in itself. Most people appreciate talent. We admire those who do excel. Most of us would rather win than lose. What is toxic about performance myths is that these achievements become a prime purpose in life and that we imagine our self-esteem as human beings is being evaluated largely by such standards.

Our natural interest in becoming more skillful and accomplished involves trial and error learning. A nourishing attitude about such efforts means the learner is primarily motivated by an interest in whatever he or she is doing while the quality of performance is at most a secondary issue. The meaning is then in the activity itself, not how well one does it.

The following dialogue occurred during a group therapy session in which Carolyn was working on her inability to get things done.

**Carolyn:** Sometimes I think I'm really stuck. There are so many things I want to do. Yet, when I get home from the office, visit with Bill (*Carolyn's husband*) and fix dinner for him and the kids, I seem to stop functioning and just sit around for the rest of the evening. I should read more. I haven't picked up my guitar in weeks. And I owe all my friends letters and thank-you notes. Beyond that, I've got a whole list of other things that are waiting to be done that I never seem to get to. Instead, I'll light up a cigarette and pour a glass of wine and sit down and watch the boob tube for two or three hours and go to bed. I guess I'm just plain lazy.

**Jackie:** I do the same thing only I don't have as good an excuse as you do. You've got a husband and two kids to take care of when you get home. When I get home there's nobody to bother me. All I have to do is fix myself something to eat and my evening is free. But I'll sit around and maybe read the newspaper, talk on the phone or watch TV while all the time in the back of my mind I know I have chores to do and I just don't feel like it.

**Dean:** You both sound like you're hassling yourselves a lot. I hear a lot of "shoulds" and I certainly do the same thing. But I found out that hassling myself and putting myself down doesn't do any good at all. It just makes me irritable and I still don't get any more done than I would otherwise. I

tell myself that, if things are really important enough to me, I'll do them and it
usually turns out that way. Sometimes I
have a deadline to meet on some work
from the office and I may procrastinate.
But at the last minute, somehow I always
manage to get it done when I really have
to.

**Carolyn:** I respond to that kind of pressure too. If
I feel someone's counting on me for something, I do get it done rather than disappoint them. I just can't stand to disappoint
someone and really get angry when people
let me down about something they promised me. So, that's kind of a different situation as I see it.

**Herb:** That's interesting. When you are left on
your own, you're lazy and when some-
one's on your back you're not lazy. That
doesn't quite make sense to me.

In this dialogue, Carolyn and Jackie get lost in self-recrimi-
nations. They try to push themselves harder yet somehow
don't get any more done. Despite their good intentions,
their pushing doesn't help at all. Carolyn lacks trust in herself. She discounts the work she does all day and, in
essence, doesn't consider her fatigue after a long day's
work acceptable. Interestingly enough, Carolyn later ack-
nowledged that on weekends she takes 40-mile bike rides
and day-long hikes and feels exhilarated afterward! As she
began to be more aware of such inconsistencies, she realized that her willingness to do things was a matter of
motivation: she never felt "lazy" when something she
found exciting was happening!

Jackie became aware that she might be sitting around not feeling like doing anything, but if her boyfriend called and asked her out she suddenly felt full of enthusiasm and energy!

Many people call themselves "lazy" when they don't feel motivated to do unpleasant chores and "shoulds." Children who don't do their homework are often called lazy by parents or teachers. Our culture implies that we must push ourselves or we won't get our work done and that, left to our own devices, we would all just sit around loafing in the sun endlessly.

## TOXIC MYTH #40
### Laziness is a natural tendency.

Trying when you really don't want to is forced behavior, whether we impose it on ourselves or allow others to impose it on us. It is a *demand* that we perform with greater effort than our motivation calls for. The you-should-try-harder ritual says we should deliberately increase the stress on ourselves in this way and that doing so is virtuous. Its implication reinforces the myth that we cannot trust ourselves, that our natural inclinations and spontaneous efforts are not sufficient. Ironically, those who are forever driving themselves to try harder usually discover that, however excellent their performance, they always feel they could have done better and rarely experience real gratification from their achievements. Far more common, they never get off their own backs and continually induce more stress on themselves by demanding greater and greater success and achievement. In essence, when they are not competing against others, they compete against themselves.

One toxic myth usually leads to another so that toxic mythology easily becomes an ever-expanding part of an individual's life. More and more rules and expectations become superimposed upon the individual when we allow ourselves to be continuously subjected to more and more "shoulds." For example, when we accept the myth that laziness is a natural tendency, we become easier prey for other myths that tell us not to trust the inner self-regulating processes that naturally motivate us to do what we feel we need to when we *really* need to. At that point (and it will come, believe it or not!) we then do it because we really want to.

**TOXIC MYTH #41**
**Competition is necessary for achievement**
**and excellence.**

Implicit in this myth is the notion that, because we fear we are naturally lazy, we need external stimuli to motive us into doing a good job or excelling. Competition per se can be an enjoyable, exhilarating experience. Games and contests of countless varieties exist in practically every known culture and often help members of the group feel closer and more caring and loving toward one another.

Like any human need, competition can be, and in our society has been, distorted into a toxic pattern over a period of time, and an elaborate toxic mythology has developed around it. The myth that competition is necessary if people are to achieve to their full potential poisons our attitude toward ourselves. We cannot trust the resources and motivations within us to enable us to reach a high level of achievement and quality of performance.

The myth that we need competition to motivate us dampens our self-initiating processes, the inner creative drive to do something well that is a natural part of every human being. To the contrary, the distrust of ourselves arouses anxiety and fear of failure when we feel we are being compared. The anxiety and stress produced by such fears, more often than not, hamper our ability to do our best. This myth also fosters a passive attitude within us. We are apt to feel that we *need* competition to motivate us. In short, it teaches us a very poisonous idea that to really do well at anything, we need someone else to turn us on, someone else to struggle against, someone else to defeat.

**TOXIC MYTH #42**
**If we can't do something well, we**
**shouldn't do it at all.**

Because achievement and success myths demand a good end product or a successful conclusion, one of their poisonous effects is to inhibit our natural inclinations to experiment with new activities and new ideas. These myths tend to inhibit us from learning by trial and error what activities suit us, what we want to commit more of our time and energy to, and what aspects of living we find most interesting.

Sometimes, of course, we discover by trial and error that what initially seemed exciting or meaningful turns out to be dull or we lose interest for other reasons. Here, too, achievement and success raise our anxiety level, for they imply that there is something wrong with dabbling in ideas and activities and then abruptly dropping them for our own reasons—or for no reason at all!

Similarly, to enjoy something and remain rather mediocre at it often creates the feeling that we should apologize for it. Those who violate the toxic ritual that we must do well at all things frequently become defensive and anxious about their mediocre skills: "I hope you'll forgive me, but I'm not very good at this." Such an attitude fosters the toxic notion that pleasure is intrinsically tied in with excellence of performance—which is another toxic attitude encouraged by this myth.

## TOXIC MYTH #43
### We should finish what we start.

When we comply with the demands for excellence made by performance myths, we give up our right to govern our own efforts and to learn and participate in what interests us. We then behave as if we have signed a contract requiring a certain level of learning and rate of improvement, which is to continue until we reach some externally determined level of excellence. Obviously, according to this myth, it is taboo to change one's mind in the middle of something, and we should feel ashamed when we leave something unfinished.

It really is not all right to read only half of a book and decide not to finish it. Most of us would feel embarrassed to admit that we have taken half a dozen guitar lessons and quit or dropped out in the middle of an adult education course. We act as if we need an excuse because it makes us look bad to state simply that we just lost interest in what we were doing.

Many of us trap ourselves with "shoulds" about the unfinished projects we have left lying around the house for months or years. The unfinished projects simply sit there creating guilt and anxiety in us as if we don't have the right to abandon such projects or throw out something half finished when we really don't want it around.

> **Joan:**   I put myself down by saying that I don't have the guts to stick to anything. That's

what always happens with me. A lot of things interest me, but only for a very short time. Then I feel empty. I try to hold on to my interest but it just gets boring. I just feel terrible, as if I've made a mistake.

**George:** (*Joan's husband*) Sometimes when I'm angry at you I try to catch you at that. When I catch you trying something new and quickly giving up, I've got you.

**Joan:** That's right! I have no way to excuse myself. I feel wiped out, empty, and like I'm a failure—and then I feel more anxious about trying something new—that again I might not want to finish or continue with.

This dialogue exemplifies the ritual that we *must* finish what we start. It is taboo not to finish something. In many ways, we swallow whole packages when part is all we want. Or, having tasted it, we realize that we don't want any more. We surrender ourselves to a ritualistic attitude that demands that we finish a book, stay until a boring party is over, eat all the food on our plate, or order dessert (especially if it comes with the meal).

## TOXIC MYTH #44
## Dabbling is Bad.

**Son:** (*age 15*) Dad, can I take tennis lessons this summer?

**Father:** I would like to say yes, but last month you asked me if you could take bowling and you quit after six lessons.

**Son:**     Well, I did learn something about bowling, but my friends quit and I got bored bowling alone.

**Father:**  That's what I mean. You young people start something and then lose interest instead of sticking with it until you become proficient.

**Son:**     I really think I'm interested in tennis. And I'm sure I'll stick with it this time.

**Father:**  Okay, I'll go along with you. But remember, I expect you to stay with it until you can really play a good game of tennis.

The father's achievement-oriented attitude is reflected in his critical remarks as he rebukes his son's approach to experimenting with what seems appealing to him. The word "dabbler" is really not as serious or conscientious as he should be. Dabbling is a kind of playing with life and expresses a light-hearted attitude frequently considered taboo. Toxic myths typically emphasize a "life-is-serious-business" attitude and frown on levity and most easygoing patterns of living.

In this dialogue, the son quite possibly might lose interest again and, despite his good intentions to be more persistent, continue vacillating back and forth among various sports indefinitely. Parents who are not stuck with achievement and performance myths are more willing to trust that their children will evolve in their own way and find their own areas of interest. In this search, external controls or penalties are more of a hindrance than a help.

Many people enjoy dabbling with various interests throughout their lives. They see no need to become proficient in everything. Eventually, they may settle into one of these activities and find that it is important to them, or they may dabble endlessly: it doesn't matter. To allow our children, and ourselves as well, to experiment in whatever way our inclinations lead is the most expedient way to discover for ourselves that a lack of external restrictions and discipline does not lead to chaos, that, quite to the contrary, it leads to a more intense, more persistent motivation because our efforts stem from choices freely made and based on our own needs and our way of responding to them, not someone else's.

**TOXIC MYTH #45**
**Achievement is more essential than experience.**

This myth is the culmination of the attitude that develops when we follow the rituals and taboos of the many variations of the competition-success-achievement myths. It teaches us that the *process* of living, the ongoing, everyday activities that compose the bulk of our lives, is secondary in importance to how it all turns out in the end. In its extreme form we are taught that the main goal of life is to one day be proclaimed a "success." All else, all our countless experiences, interactions with other people, pleasures and frustrations, all of the processes that make us human and are the essence of life itself are relegated to a secondary position. Those who fall victim to this poisonous myth and achieve "success" in their middle or later years frequently become extremely depressed, angry or apathetic when they discover how much of their life they have lost because they swallowed the myth that experiencing life is not as important as what you make of yourself.

When we observe many of the outstanding citizens of our society and have even a moderate exposure to what their life-style is really like and how they react to it, we discover that these people are not any more joyous or content, or any less tense and irritable than the rest of us. What often happens to "winners" is that, because each achievement fails to bring the hoped-for gratification, they continue to reach for greater heights, more success, additional accomplishments, always in the hope that finally they will feel the satisfaction of fulfillment. For example, the main use of wealth for the achiever is to generate more wealth. Gradually the need for achievement evolves into a need for power. Wealth is used to influence and manipulate other people. The struggle for power has no end and is insatiable. Seen in this perspective, the achievement-success orientation easily becomes a treadmill to oblivion for those who are most accomplished.

### ATHLETICS: YOU'RE EITHER A WINNER OR A LOSER

Our attitude about athletics and "physical education" exemplifies the compulsive rituals of our society that demand that every school child—fat or thin, muscular or frail, interested or not—compete to win. Ritual demands that everyone strive for athletic achievement, and it is taboo to quit or to refuse to try.

Anyone can visit a school playground during a gym class and see boys and girls walking away from their "failure" with their heads hanging down in shame. These are the same children doomed to fail in competitive games. They are consistently picked last and given the least desirable positions and the least amount of attention by the teacher. They are a classic example of the victims of forced competition. They are the "losers" being taught that only "winners" are really acceptable.

### EVERYBODY IS AFRAID HE OR SHE IS MISSING SOMETHING: MORE IS BETTER

The success myth promises that the more material abundance, social status or other culturally approved achievements we acquire, the more our lives will be enriched. This perpetuates the lie that quantity always does equal meaningfulness.

*No one* knows what goes on inside us but ourselves. We imagine that the accomplished person feels good about life. This myth poisons us with the unnecessary pain of culturally conceived expectations when we discover that success does not yield the total gratification we have been led to believe it should. Often the achiever wonders, "What's wrong with me that my pleasure at my accomplishments is so short-lived? Why doesn't my success mean more to me?"

Sometimes we play the role of a "success" to fulfill the expectations of others and to avoid facing our own disillusionment. The toxic myth that "more is better" then becomes a life-style of increasing stress and tension resulting from the futile and endless struggle to be more and then more successful.

> At 43, Glen was a successful attorney who, for a number of years, as far as anyone could tell, had enjoyed the fruits of his endeavors. He and his wife lived in a lovely home with their three children. Their home was a social center and scarcely a week passed without their entertaining at least once or twice.
>
> Most other evenings, Glen was occupied attending other social functions, or participating as a member of various civic communities. No one paid attention to his excessive drinking, and those who did felt he was entitled to indulge himself because he had done so much for the community and represented an outstanding model of success.

Only his wife knew of the many days he was so depressed that it took all the energy he could muster to get out of bed and face the endless obligations that lay before him. Yet as he walked out the front door each morning carrying his briefcase and wearing an expensive suit, he was, for all the world to see, an outstanding example of a well-adjusted, happy, admirable human being. His chronic ulcer was often a source of humor as his friends laughingly suggested that maybe he needed to see a shrink. Glen felt he was stuck with maintaining this image and demanded of himself a continuously outstanding performance that would meet the expectations of everyone and avoid any criticism or rebuke.

For years he had had suicidal impulses that he would not share even with his wife. With her, too, he lived under the fear that if she really knew of his inner agony, she, too, would be disappointed and lose the respect and esteem she held for him.

His wife was totally bewildered when he left the house early one morning, before anyone was awake, leaving a note telling her of his desperation and that he saw no solution but to take his own life. Two days later, his body was found in a nearby city. He had taken an overdose of sedatives and had been dead for over 24 hours.

The fact that this rat race generated by the competition-success-achievement myths takes its toll is obvious. The enormous use of drugs, sleeping pills, tranquilizers and alcohol may be more frequent among successful achievers than it is among the rest of us—and is probably more so.

We refuse to confront ourselves with the facts that the unnatural stress in our achievement-oriented culture is a primary reason for our need to escape, at least temporarily, by artificial means.

In past eras, when we were less dependent on one another for our personal survival, competition was perhaps less toxic. Now our competitive attitudes are becoming increasingly obsolete and are creating increasing numbers of social problems. Success and competition myths still perpetuate the "room-at-the-top" kind of endless ritualistic struggle: work harder, try harder, don't be a quitter, and so forth. In this way, a no-win environment in which more and more people are trapped by realistic frustrations is created and encouraged. People who feel they are "losers" have little realistic opportunity to do anything about it. Blocked at every turn, many allow their frustrations to explode in antisocial behavior (I'll steal to succeed) or implode (explode inwardly) as they turn to drugs or alcohol, or become apathetic about themselves and their existence.

Competition or striving to achieve excellence is not in itself toxic and can be nourishing to both the individual and society. It is *how* we use these attitudes that makes them so poisonous. When we get caught up with achieving success, we tend to become obsessed and locked into a narrow view about the meaning of life and our whole existence in this world. The real sadness of those caught up in the success-achievement myths is that they never allow themselves to experience the many dimensions of life and the many possible meanings and levels of awareness that do exist within all human beings. They settle for very little compared to what is potentially available when we allow ourselves to be caught in the competition-success-achievement myths of our society.

Those who feel they must struggle to reach the mountaintop of success and achievement, typically miss the experience of living each day to its fullest. Instead, we focus our attention and interest and gratification on future goals. We are further disconnected from ourselves to the extent that our rewards are externally oriented and based on recognition from others. Such preoccupation keeps us from experiencing our inner essence.

## YOU DON'T HAVE TO PLAY THE GAME
Part of the antidote process in remedying this dilemma is to begin to see what an enormous price we pay when we commit ourselves to the competition-success-achievement myth. We drain ourselves physically, emotionally and spiritually when we become obsessed with the promises of this toxic mythology. Heart attacks are the common plague of middle-aged executives. Usually the physical effects are not so dramatic and take the form of chronic feelings of fatigue, lack of energy, lack of motivation or a seemingly insatiable need for rest and relaxation.

We also need to be aware that often the means of relieving stress and strain are in themselves poisonous, both physically and emotionally, to our well-being. The psychic anesthesias, drugs, tranquilizers and alcohol that so many millions of people depend on to keep going are not without their detrimental effects and all too frequently create new tensions and problems, which in themselves can be quite devastating. We can begin to question what it is that we do that causes us to need drugs, tranquilizers or alcohol. We can become aware of the loneliness we create for ourselves when we look at those around us as competitors or as hostile forces from which we believe we must protect ourselves.

There is a certain social approval, or at least a lack of social disapproval, for the use of drugs, alcohol and tranquilizers by those who are struggling for success and achievement. It's okay for them. After all, look how hard they work! Look how much responsibility they have! In contrast, the skid row wino does not have the same sanction. Because he is anything but a hard-driving achiever, his use of drugs and alcohol only adds to his unacceptability. Alcoholism is the socially approved escape from emotional tension for those who have achieved the most and are the most successful.

Focusing life goals on becoming successful competitors is probably a dominant theme in the lives of most people. Most of us would include material success and recognition of our achievements and social status as major components of what the "good life" means to us. In our society the tendency is to acknowledge that physical health, loving relationships and contributing to peace and the welfare of humankind are essential aspects of the "good life." For most of us, such acknowledgments turn out to be well-meaning lip service. Adults spend most of their time and energy working to provide for their material needs, to provide a home for themselves and their families and, in general, to obtain some degree of emotional and economic security. In actuality, these needs are filled for most of us. Most of us have a home, food, clothes, love, and so on. (True, a minority of people do not and this cannot be denied, but it could be remedied in a society as affluent as ours.)

Yet when we look around at others or look inwardly at ourselves, discontentment, anxiety, fear and insecurity are clearly what is most apparent. "Successful" people don't seem to look happy, act happy or feel happy. The toxic myths that foster the competition-success-achievement rat race account for much of how we cheat ourselves and others out of the joys of living and appreciating what life has given us. We tend to exist day-by-day as if we were deaf, dumb and blind as we focus on what is undone or unfinished, and on what goals or conquests we should direct our attention to. It seems that most of us only appreciate what we have after we have lost it through some tragedy or other circumstance.

## We can alter this grim attitude toward life by letting go of our future-oriented life-style.

What this means is letting go of the success-achievement rat race and the endless onward-and-upward driving of ourselves. To illustrate the attitude implicit in this approach, let us consider the way most of us look at work and play.

A society in which the individual is taught to survive and excel by defeating others defeats itself in the process. We literally create generations in which the majority are losers.

"Losers" are usually angry, alienated and frustrated. They are trapped in a continuing struggle in the hope that eventually they will be able to disregard their stigma and subsequently reach first-class citizen status. On the other hand, the relatively few who do succeed are often stuck with a continuous struggle to maintain a position by fighting off challengers or continuing to climb further up, achieving more and more. For these people also there is no end to the struggle because they might slip and become a "has-been," a particularly shameful kind of loser.

We can also become aware of the many kinds of nourishing experiences we deprive ourselves of, often knowingly and willingly, because of our overwhelming drive for success. We can become aware when we don't allow time for our own solitude, for being with those we love and for experiencing more of ourselves. The more we see the many ways in which we pay the price for being success-oriented, the more it can help us to at least modify these kinds of goals and keep them in a more reasonable perspective in terms of our total existence.

The tension of the rat race loosens when we decide to let go of our role in playing these kinds of self-manipulating games and turn inwardly towards ourselves to become more aware of what we need. In this way we free our energy for a greater expression of ourselves in other dimensions of life and other aspects of our humanness.

Returning to our natural process of growth will ultimately bring out a creative expression and the discovery of more of our own potential. In this way we are more likely to become aware of the many levels of consciousness and the many dimensions of physical, emotional and spiritual life available to all of us when we turn our attention to them, and we can do this without having to compete with anyone or succeed in anything.

Letting go of anything poisonous is in itself a nourishing act. Such acts are usually accompanied by a feeling of relief followed by a resurgence of energy and excitement. This process becomes easier as we become more aware of how distorted our perceptions are of the "winners" or successful people. What we see is their achievements. What we don't see is *them*. We may see their riches or the recognition and acclaim others bestow, but this tells us nothing of their inner being, fears, anxieties and insecurities, or their lack of lovingness or feeling loved. Envy is invariably our own projection of our limited perception of another person as a whole human being.

Another antidote to the competition-success-achievement game is to appreciate more fully that all of us struggle in our own way and experience our own pains of various kinds that are not affected one way or the other by how well we do in the achievement rat race. When we see this rat race as a detour, it can help us return to the only reality *we have on this earth:* the here-and-now. Emotional nourishment is only in the present. Focusing on the here-and-now gives meaning and aliveness to our activities as we experience them for ourselves, not as means toward some future goal. In contrast, the drive for success is future-oriented and, like most things we fantasize about in the future, is apt to fill us with anxiety and fear. Living in the now simplifies our lives. We actually need less and experience more ongoing gratifications from what is. The present is always full of excitement and meaning if we will only look. The future is fantasy and at best leaves us hoping we will eventually discover the meaningfulness and joy of living which surrounds us now but is blurred by our headlong race toward success and achievement.

## Myths About Work and Play

A longstanding attitude prevails about work and play which causes us to sort most of what we do into one category or the other. Each time we do so, most of us automatically impose on ourselves a pattern of attitudes that strongly influences our expectations about what various activities will mean to us (e.g., pleasant or unpleasant) *before* we actually experience them. We expect "work" to be unpleasant or burdensome, something we are glad to be finished with. We expect "play" to be exciting and joyful, something we don't want to come to an end. In this way we are taught to look at work and play as qualitatively different, mutually exclusive kinds of activities.

## TOXIC MYTH #46
**Play is a luxury.**

Toxic myths about play originated in an era when survival required a continuous physical struggle throughout our lives. Activities that were not productive toward physical and economic survival were socially frowned upon. Play is still considered by many as largely a form of self-indulgence. Because it is nonproductive in that it does not produce any concrete results or achievement, it is considered to be something we legitimately have a right to enjoy only after our work is completed.

## TOXIC MYTH #47
**Work is virtuous.**

In contrast to play, we are taught that work is a burden we must grimly bear, usually for the sole purpose of meeting our material needs. Compared to play, work is considered a more noble activity. Participating in it makes better persons of us and makes us more socially acceptable.

Myths about work perpetuate the attitude that those activities we label as "work" are inherently distasteful, but that this is compensated for by the virtuous feelings and material gain they provide.

## TOXIC MYTH #48
**A hard worker is a "good" person and**
**"good people" are hard workers.**

Comparing work and play exemplifies the artificial categories toxic myths create. Almost any activity that has been called work by some has been chosen by others for interest and enjoyment. Labeling something "work" distorts the reality that it is not what we do but how we experience it that determines our attitude about the effort we expend.

Myths about work and play cause us to rank our needs according to their social desirability rather than according to our personal desires. While work and play are both essential needs for most of us, the "slave to his/her job" is accepted and admired while the playboy/girl is frowned upon (and envied) for having found some way to avoid work. Although most of us would probably choose to play more and work less, some degree of guilt is usually felt for having this preference.

A more natural (less toxic) attitude toward work would consider it an activity we feel we must do when there are other things we would prefer to do. Work, then, means engaging in less exciting or interesting activities in terms of our spontaneous feelings about what we would prefer at the moment. Instead of allowing us to be self-regulating about these priorities, toxic myths about work use guilt and shame to coerce us into doing what *should* be done.

## TOXIC MYTH #49
**First we should do our work and, if we do a good enough job, we have earned the right to play.**

Toxic myths about work and play are another offshoot of the onward-and-upward achievement myths discussed previously. In this respect, not only is the hard worker considered a better person, but the nourishing, life-giving qualities of playful activities are ignored. Toxic myths about work and play sustain the concept that toiling endlessly throughout one's life is "better" than working less and choosing to spend time enjoying recreation, art, music or other interests. The virtuous attitude of the hard worker myths cause us to view as self-indulgent those interested in experiencing as much of life as possible. After all, according to this more limited viewpoint, there is little to show for our effort when we engage in activities primarily for the meaningfulness of the experience rather than for concrete, productive results.

The antidote to the toxic myths about work and play begins with letting go of our preconceived notions that the purpose of what we are doing and the results of these activities determine whether they are joyful or burdensome. When we let go of the unreal dichotomy with which we separate work from play, we will discover that almost any activity has its pleasant and unpleasant aspects. This antidote process becomes even more effective when we give up judging what we do as either virtuous or self-centered or that one kind of activity is better than another and instead live our lives by simply being more responsive to our ongoing flow of needs. With this more normal attitude we simply respond to these needs we feel are most urgent at the time and move on from there.

**THE GLORIES OF RETIREMENT**

In a sense, toxic myths about the dichotomous nature of work and play culminate in our concept of retirement: we never have to work again! Ritual has it that we are expected to respond joyfully and with tremendous relief, as if a great burden had been suddenly lifted from our shoulders.

> Everyone expected Ted to go places during his life. He was popular throughout his childhood years and was one of the star athletes in school. He had always known he was ambitious and was determined to be successful. At the end of his second year in college he was offered a job with a large chain of shoe stores with the promise that, within a short time, he would be manager and from there he could move up within the company.

Ted found the work as a shoe salesman tedious and boring; however, he stuck it out and in six months was transferred to another store as assistant manager. A year later he became manager and continued in that position for the next five years. During that time he came to know some of the top executives of the company. They sent him to various business and management training seminars and courses and assured him that his future with the company was very bright. He was 29 when he was promoted to district manager in charge of 18 stores. Ted put in longer and longer hours. Each step up the ladder seemed to make him more ambitious than ever.

Ted had married and when their second child was born, he and his wife moved into a home in an upper-middle-class suburb. He really began to feel that the good life was his. He was still in his thirties when the company offered him a position with the home office. This was the break he had been waiting for. Now he would be spending his time with top management and he saw an unlimited future awaiting him. It meant selling their home and moving to another city where the executive headquarters and main manufacturing facilities were located. The transition—leaving all their friends and making a new life—was not easy for his children and his wife.

The other executives in the company welcomed Ted and his family. Their circle of new friends became largely other executives within the same company. They purchased a large house in an elegant suburb and the children went to the best private schools.

By most people's standards, Ted would now be considered successful. He held a very high position within a large company, had accumulated capital for some outside investments, and had economic security for himself and his family. Nevertheless, Ted was as ambitious as ever. It was quite a shock to Ted that a vice-presidency for which he was being considered went to someone else. Ted had started with the company right out of college and had been with them for 25 years. Now in his late forties, the job was given to a man several years younger because the Board of Directors had decided that the stress involved in this position might be too much for Ted. Until then he had never considered his age any handicap whatsoever. In fact, he had felt his maturity would be an asset in terms of future promotions to the highest levels within the company.

Ted went into a rather severe depression as he began to realize that he had reached the peak of his success and that he really wasn't going any further. Feeling stuck in his present position in the company, he decided to use the money he had accumulated to take greater risks in outside business ventures. He knew the shoe business inside and out, but he knew very little else. His experience had always been quite narrow and the investments he chose were in other areas. These ventures failed and dissipated the capital he had spent years accumulating.

Ted had considered leaving the company but now was stuck. Jobs at all comparable to his were difficult to find for a man in his early fifties. Now it was just a matter of waiting for mandatory retirement which, according to company policy, was at age 65. To Ted's embarrassment, the traditional company dinner took place at his retirement. He received the traditional gold watch and the good wishes of everyone. He left angry, depressed and unbelieving. The experience itself seemed to him like a "B" movie he had watched a hundred times during his life.

The next day he awoke, but there was no place to go. For a while he kept in touch with his friends at the company, but found that he had lost interest in their preoccupation with the company. He had a comfortable retirement plan because of his many years with the company, and he his wife began to travel. Ted enjoyed traveling, but gradually began to feel emptier and emptier. The children were grown and married and now Ted and his wife were alone in a house much too large for them. They didn't really want to leave it, but the expenses were too much. They sold their home and bought a condominium in a retirement community. Ted was bored, restless and increasingly irritable. It was a struggle to fill his time with sports and recreational activities. The emptiness was overwhelming and Ted became more withdrawn, lethargic and apathetic. Five years later, after a short illness, he died of cancer.

In our culture, material gratification is the principal reward for a lifetime of work which, more often than not, has been largely tedious and boring. It is not surprising, then, that our mythology promises that eventually we will be released from this burden and be free to finally enjoy the good life we have always heard about but never found. For those who continue to fail to achieve the goals of material success and social status, and still cling to the long-promised rewards such achievements would bring, the retirement myth gives hope of at least finding a mini-pot of gold at the end of the rainbow before our life in this world ends.

## TOXIC MYTH #50
## With aging comes a natural longing for retirement.

The sudden transition from work to formal or forced retirement is, in itself, an unnatural happening for healthy people at any age. Toxic myths glorify retirement by presenting a picture of the retired person as happily engaged in the pursuit of hobbies, travel and recreation. The ritual demands that people in their sixties and older who are vigorous and in good health should suddenly and joyfull shift from a daily schedule of work, which for several decades has utilized a large portion of their time and energy, to a dip in the pool, a little shuffleboard, a walk in the night and other random activities.

## TOXIC MYTH #51
## We should expect to enjoy retirement even when it is forced upon us.

While recreational activities may be enjoyable and can become a life-style, they fail to provide the sustenance necessary for a meaningful existence for most elderly people. Within a year or two, after the retired person has had time to vacation and catch up on things, he or she is apt to feel a kind of retirement "shock" when the expectations of a lifelong dream bear the bitter fruit of uselessness, loneliness and futility. Usually there is no sudden crisis. Rather, a gradual psychic poisoning occurs from the lack of meaning, the feeling of not being needed and, perhaps most important, a feeling of no longer contributing something of value to his or her world.

The retired person's aliveness wanes, both emotionally and physically. The effect is subtle. The illnesses and disabilities that now appear are easily attributed to age. The ritual of retirement at a specified, arbitrary age is toxic to those elderly people who don't want to be removed from the mainstream of the work-a-day world. As in all toxic myths, ritual takes precedence over individual needs and individual differences.

The poisonous effects of the retirement myth are enhanced when we are misled into believing that we no longer need to exert effort and initiative to make life meaningful and keep it that way. Because most of us throughout our lives relish vacations with release from everyday routine and obligations, it is often difficult to imagine that we could ever have too much of such freedom.

**Work and a feeling of being valued and
needed are basic human needs.**

Retirement myths hamper our ability to plan a meaningful life when this usually sudden, drastic change in the life-style does occur. The "glories-of-retirement" myth often dupes people into a life of unnecessary discontent. We cannot allow it to con us into thinking that at long last our worries will be over. We should plan on an alternate life-style, which may take years to discover, to which we can adapt as retirement approaches.

Is This
Really
What I Want
To Do
With

My Sex Life

## Myths About Sex

From the beginning our society has been obsessed with sexuality. Until the turn of the century this preoccupation was largely focused on keeping the subject in the realm of secret knowledge. Obviously, with such secrecy, taboos about sex were rampant. It was considered taboo even to talk about sex. And it was not unusual for married couples to avoid nudity even during intercourse. Yet these practices did little to lessen the intensity of sexual feelings and may have made them stronger.

Many myths, taboos and rituals about sex dating back hundreds of years continue to have a powerful effect on our present-day attitudes, despite the fact that most teenagers and adults are knowledgeable about the basics of sex and reproduction. The persistent power of toxic myths, based on deeply ingrained beliefs handed down from generation to generation, does not disappear with increased enlightenment. The availability of knowledge about human sexuality is not enough to change emotional attitudes quickly.

We are not only the victims of centuries-old myths about sex, but of new myths, taboos and rituals as well. The latter come into being during the so-called sexual revolution that began with World War II and have evolved into new forms of preoccupation with sex.

What has happened is what psychologists call a reaction formation: A movement from one extreme to the other. We have moved from the inhibition, prudishness and secrecy of the Victorian era to a total openness and a no-holds-barred attitude toward sex. This counter revolution advances the attitude that sex in practically any form with anyone is totally acceptable and is the private business of the individual participants.

## TOXIC MYTH #52
### Sexual inhibitions mean we are neurotic.

The sexual freedom movement seems to be gradually releasing us from the repressive, anxiety- and neurosis-producing effects of the Victorian era. But accompanying this sexual freedom is a new list of taboos and rituals, enforced with the same social pressure behind all toxic myths. Now we are made to feel guilty or ashamed when we fail to live up to the expectations and demands of the new sexual mores. For example, now we are apt to feel guilty if we avoid sex or feel inhibited under any circumstances. Under the new rules of sexual freedom, inhibition is taboo.

The following conversation took place during a group therapy session. The participants were discussing their feelings, anxieties and insecurities about sex and dating:

**Cindy:** (*Age 20*) This dating is really getting to be a pain in the ass. I knew this was going to happen when I broke up with John (*whom Cindy had dated exclusively for two years*). In fact, many times when I knew that our relationship wasn't going anywhere, I still talked myself into continuing to see him because I dreaded the idea of turning up at a local meat market (*singles bar*). I'm still looking for a one-to-one relationship with a future, but I know that when I go out with one of these guys, he is going to try to get me into bed on the first date for sure. Usually when I tell a date that I like him, but I'd like to get to know him better first, he lays this guilt trip on me: "What's the matter, are you inhibited or something?"

**Diane:** You must be reading my mind! I had to laugh when you said that dating was a pain in the ass. I never thought of it that way, but it's true. I used to think it was supposed to be fun and exciting to meet new guys, and maybe find someone who really turns me on and that I could really relate to. But mostly I find the same thing: when I like the guy, can I hold him off from getting me into bed on the first date without his getting angry and never calling me again. If I don't like the guy, it's no problem. He can get lost and that's okay. But I hate to go to bed with a guy just because we had a good time together and I like him, even if he turns me on. When I talk about this with my girlfriends, I usually get the same old response: "Well, if you like him and he turns you on, why not go to bed with him?"

**Vera:** Call me old-fashioned if you want, but I don't go for this ritual that, when two people turn each other on, it means they should automatically go to bed right away. I still like to see whether we really have a broader basis for a relationship. But I find that, if I just respond because some guy turns me on sexually, the relationship usually stays at that level and

when the sexual excitement of the new relationship begins to subside, someone
leaves.

**Sam:** What you women are saying is really a
revelation to me. I have to laugh at myself
because I'm uptight every time I go out
with a new woman. I'm afraid that, if we
like each other, she'll expect me to try to
get her in bed and if I don't, she'll think
I'm weird or something (*laughter*).

**Carl:** I think you all have sexual hang-ups.
What's the big deal about two people sharing their bodies with each other? Myself,
I'm a swinger. There's this place I go to
where we have nude encounter groups
and marathons and it's really beautiful —
no inhibitions, no guilt, everybody just full
of love and expressing it. If you don't want
to participate, you don't have to. Nobody
gets uptight about that either. We just go
around naturally doing what we feel. A lot
of us are into making love without getting
involved in some deep relationships or
making promises nobody intends to keep.
I used to have a line to try to seduce
women into going to bed with me. Now
I'm much more honest. I just ask them if
they would like to screw and if they say
yes, fine; if not, there are plenty of other
chicks around who will.

**Cindy:** That's what I mean. You're the kind of guy
who, if I said to you, "I like you, but I
don't want to go to bed with you," would
think I was square. You think women
should look at sex as if you were just invit-

ing them to a coffee shop for a hamburger. If you're hungry, you take up the invitation; if you're not, you say, "No thanks, I'm not hungry." Well, sex means a lot more to me than that.

**Carl:**  Wow! Are you ever hung up! Sometime you should come with me to one of my weekend nude marathons and then see where you are at.

**Vera:**  Carl, you really turn me off. You think sex makes the world go around. You can't see a relationship any further than the end of your organ. Quite honestly, I don't have much respect for you, and I don't think you have any respect for women. For you they're just a piece of meat; a way for you to get rid of your sexual tensions and nothing more.

**Carl:**  I sure wouldn't want to make it with you. You're not a bad-looking chick, but that's sure an old-fashioned number you sound like you're stuck with. For me, I like a chick who wants to make it three or four times a day.

**George:**  Come on, Carl, aren't you putting it on a little heavy? (*Carl laughs with a smirk on his face.*)

**Fred:**  I used to belong to a swingers' group and it was really groovy. Me and my ex-wife would meet with this group and ball all weekend. Sometimes it was dark and you didn't even know who you were balling. Now that's sexual freedom—no hang-ups. You just do your own thing. I think everybody would be swingers if they weren't scared or afraid that they would be inadequate. Me, I feel more like Carl.

## THE NEW SEX MYTHOLOGY

Myths about sex have now become a two-way bind for many people. First we were caught in the Victorian tradition with its attitude that sex is bad, something to be repressed and avoided as much as possible.

## THE TABOO AGAINST SEXUAL MODESTY

The newer sexual rituals encourage us to be totally open sexually to anyone of our choosing. Modesty is viewed as some carry-over in a person who has not yet reached full sexual enlightenment.

## TOXIC MYTH #53

**Having sex is normal and healthy, so
there is no reason not to have sex
whenever and with whomever you want.**

Most people who consider themselves "hip" would accept this statement, expecially if we qualify it by adding that some contraceptive measure has been taken to prevent pregnancy. This "why-not" attitude places sexual appetites on the same level as our desires for food, rest and recreation and is expressed in the question: Why *not* do it if you feel like it?

## THE SEXUAL PROVING GROUND

In what is yet another version of the success-achievement myths discussed previously, the new sex mythology is very powerful when it comes to the question of what it means to be a "real man" or a "real woman". This is another version of the success-achievement myths discussed previously. We are taught that we must strive to achieve status as a "real man" or a "real woman" and if we fail, we will be labeled as inadequate. As a result, its victims, in actuality, millions of men and women, live out their lives full of secret fear and anxiety that they are not sexually what they should be.

## FOXIE

"Foxie" is a popular label that we will use here for the mythical "real woman" in our society. Foxie is young and gorgeous, has large breasts and a thin waistline, and is somewhat underweight. Her sexual success lies not necessarily in terms of conquests but rather in the availability to her of desirable males—those who are sexually most attractive, as well as those who are successful achievers in various fields, fame, wealth, etc.

## TOXIC MYTH #54
**Foxie women have a stronger sex drive
than ordinary women.**

## Jock

"Jock" is a frequent label for the mythical "real man" in our society. He is physically handsome with broad shoulders and narrow hips. His penis is presumed to be larger than average, and he is expected to be a sexual athlete who can perform on demand to the satisfaction of any woman. When a woman is not satisfied sexually, Jock, of course, insists that it is her hang-up, not his. Typically, our mythical "real man" considers it a challenge to be able to seduce (conquer) any woman he finds attractive, especially those who resist his charms. He is the successful sexual achiever just as the millionaire is the successful economic achiever. The mythical attitude about jocks is that they have special qualities that make them different from and superior to "ordinary men."

## TOXIC MYTH #55
### Jocks have a stronger sex drive than ordinary men.

Such superman mythology views Jock as a Casanova who goes from woman to woman in an endless succession of glorious new seductions, which are necessary to satisfy his alleged superior sex drive. New conquests are a ritualistic aspect of the "real man" myth so that it is taboo for him to remain with any one woman. While he may romantically return to old loves, these encounters are brief, ending in glorious farewells. The mythical role of the woman in this drama is that, while she may be jealous or angry about his philandering, she always melts at his advances and is delighted to be with him and to please him any way she can!

## TOXIC MYTH #56
### People who are sexually attractive are more passionate and enjoy sex more.

Our mythical "real man" and "real woman" have sexuality on their mind most of the time, or they should have. Their masculinity and femininity are measured by the intensity of their sexual desires and the frequency with which these are fulfilled. Their very preoccupation with their sexuality is considered to be a valid indication that they are sexually mature and enlightened.

## TOXIC MYTH #57
## Younger people enjoy sex more than
## older people and are more passionate.

Like the myths fostered by Victorian attitudes, which are still very active and powerful, these newer myths also distort our natural sexuality by their excessive preoccupation with performance. Their poisonous effect is seen in the anxieties, insecurities and fears they foster in millions of adults whose only "sex problem" is that they have been manipulated by our toxic mythology about sex into believing that they have sex problems. In this intimate aspect of our personal lives, we see an example of how toxic myths can make deep intrusions into our privacy. The degree to which almost all of us have been victimized by these myths is evident in this dialogue:

**Jock:** (*Paying the check as he and his date get ready to leave the restaurant after their first date*) Let's go to my place. I've got some records you'll really dig.

**Prudish Penny:** Well, um — I don't know about that —

**Jock:** What's the matter, baby? You're not one of those uptight chicks, are you? You looked hip to me or I wouldn't have dated you in the first place.

**Penny:** Well, I'd like to get to know a man for a while before I go to his apartment. Can't we go dancing or something?

**Jock:** Look, baby, you're just marking time. There are lots of girls just dying to make it with me. Haven't you heard of my reputation about town?

**Penny:** I'm really feeling pressured. We hardly know each other.

**Jock:** Well, we have to start someplace, don't we? Sex is the best way there is for us to get to know each other. What harm can come of it?

**Penny:** I guess I'm old-fashioned, but I'm just too nervous.

**Jock:** Okay! There's no point in our rapping about it anymore. I don't have any patience with prudes. I'm sorry you are not hip sexually. You don't know what you're missing!

In this dialogue, Jock sees himself as a sexual success. He is the personification of the achiever in the sexual area. His behavior is ritualistic with an automatic take-it-for-granted attitude toward Penny. For him, the ritual is that each woman goes to bed with him or there is no way to continue the relationship. Jock has little tolerance for any protests against having sex, no matter how Penny feels about it. His attitude shows him to be a victim of the anti-Victorian mythology, who needs to rebel against all sexual inhibitions and cannot tolerate any woman whose attitude about sex differs from his in the slightest.

As with other success-achievement myths, the sexual success, whether one is male or female, is most apt to create a feeling of bewilderment, depression or emptiness about his or her sexuality, for while they are successful, the excitement and adventure gradually wane as each relationship begins to feel increasingly similar to the one before and the one before that, and the conquests and sex itself become monotonous. It is not unusual for sexual achievers to begin to feel that going to bed with one person is the same as going to bed with another, that they are all just so many bodies. This is most apt to be the case when relationships remain on the superficial level of physical gratification only.

The same is true of those women who have liberated themselves sexually and enjoy sex with an unending series of new men. Often they are so convinced that their sexual enlightenment can only be good, that they fail to see its poisonous effects in preventing them from discovering the deeper aspects of intimate relating between the sexes.

The fact is that millions of sexually free men and women often feel depressed, embarrassed, even disgusted as they look at each other the next morning. But both will insist that everything is cool and, in keeping with the ritual of the "hip people," they each go their separate ways.

Those who seek to win the coveted label of "real man" or "real woman" can easily lose themselves in their quest for sexual success. They are also prone to be further poisoned by another taboo: jocks and foxes tend to be handicapped in developing love relationships with one person or surrendering to a growing one-to-one intimacy when it spontaneously evolves. For to limit one's sexuality to a single person, shoots down all the glorious struggles for the ritualistic achievements that require continuous variety and new sexual conquests.

## Victorian Mythology

**TOXIC MYTH #58**
**The body is evil.**

This myth is based on the more encompassing one that the higher levels of human development are more easily attained when we ignore or denounce the pleasures of the body. It forms the basis for numerous taboos and rituals about sex and other bodily functions. These taboos teach us to be ashamed of natural bodily functions, and maintain that the body itself is dirty and a dangerous source of taboo temptations.

## TOXIC MYTH #59
## Body contact is the same as sexual contact.

> Barry was a loving father who enjoyed his children and appreciated them as individuals. Members of his family expressed affection openly, were physically demonstrative and had always felt comfortable being nude in front of one another. When Barry became aware that his oldest daughter's breasts were beginning to develop, he became anxious and flustered. He began to feel uneasy about physical contact with her, would no longer kiss her on the lips, and when they hugged, was careful to avoid body contact, especially near the genital area.

The taboo against body contact between males is particularly strong in our culture. While it is more socially acceptable for women to embrace, hold hands and kiss in public, even accidental contact between males is apt to elicit embarrassed apologies from both parties. Physical affection between men remains taboo because of the myth that such expressions may imply some homosexual intent. Homosexuality still remains a strict taboo for both sexes in spite of more liberal attitudes and greater openness among those who prefer this kind of sexual relationship.

## TOXIC MYTH #60
**Sexual pleasures promote decadence.**

This lie warns us that excessive indulgence in sexual pleasures will corrupt our abilities as responsible, caring
members of society. The admonition that a sexually free
attitude leads to a life-style of orgies for the "fallen"
individual implies that our sexual appetite (unlike any other
body need) is insatiable.


## TOXIC MYTH #61
**The primary factor determining how our
personality and behavior as individual
human beings will evolve is whether we
are male or female.**

Myths about sex are toxic when they imply that gender is
the prime factor in determining a particular person's character and qualities as a human being, or mode of relating
to others and to the world in general. Myths that place a
person's gender in a primary role are intrinsically toxic and
reflect obsolete attitudes ignoring the reality that, first and
foremost, each of us is a human being. These myths generate endless conflicts by artificially differentiating acceptable and unacceptable behavior according to gender. They
sanction, demand or prohibit certain acts and attitudes
solely on the basis of sex. For example, many people of
both sexes still blindly follow the ritual that only men
should initiate sex and that women should only respond to
men's sexual overtures. Further, according to this toxic ritual, if she is a "real woman" she should always be recep-
tive. Similarly, many men feel it is taboo to be disinterested when a woman does express her sexual interest first.

Men often fear that their disinterest at that time would reflect badly on their masculinity or even their virility.

## TOXIC MYTH #62
## There is a natural rivalry between the sexes.

Numerous myths reflect the common belief that there is a natural rivalry between the sexes. The prime importance of each person as an individual is subordinated to the mythical "battle between the sexes." The struggle between the sexes is ritualistically initiated in the prevalent attitudes of most parents who relate differently to their children according to gender. The first question most of us ask when a child is born is whether it is a boy or a girl. Then we inquire about the infant's health, weight, and so on.

Such rituals set the stage for a toxic battle between the sexes, as if an individual's struggle for emotional satisfaction and fulfillment makes combat with the opposite sex inevitable. Rather than a natural or inevitable phenomenon, this rivalry is strictly one of our culture's myths. For example, the term "castrating female" and slang expressions to this effect have become household words. They are popular weapons used by many men when rejected sexually. They reflect the toxic taboo that prohibits a woman from "making a man feel inadequate." The same myth is applied to women who compete with men economically. If they demonstrate their competence or excel at their jobs, they are considered emasculating and seen as conspiring against men. Damning a woman who succeeds can free a man from taking responsibility for his own inadequacies and dealing with his frustrations. Many women act apologetic if their incomes exceed those of their husbands. Similarly, many men are particularly bad

losers when it happens to be a woman (wife, lover or otherwise) who defeats them in some game or sport.

**TOXIC MYTH #63**
**Men are superior to women.**

**TOXIC MYTH #64**
**Men need to feel superior to women.**

Despite the progress of the feminist movement, these
myths are still dominant and are manifested in the countless ways we react differently to each sex from birth. For
example, even in early childhood, boys are ritualistically
taught to control their emotions, including their needs to
express feelings of affection, fear or anxiety or other emotions. For the little girls, in contrast, the mythical attitude
remains that while "emotions are bad, what can you expect
from a girl!" This double standard of rituals and taboos
carries over into adulthood. Many women still believe such
myths as, when they become more emotional in an argument with a man, it means they are losing the argument;
they should be "strong" like the man and suppress their
emotions.

In sexual intercourse, the Victorian attitude still persists
that:

**TOXIC MYTH #65**
**Sex is something a man does to a woman.**

The corollary of this myth is the attitude expressed by
many women that:

**Sex is something a woman allows a man
to do to her.**

These myths obviously enhance the sense of rivalry between the sexes and encourage man and woman to relate to each other, not as two people, but as opponents whose gratifications in many areas are only possible at the expense of the other.

## TOXIC MYTH #66
## Women have more sexual problems than men do.

This sexist attitude stems directly from the body of Victorian mythology about female sexuality. A woman was expected to submit to sex for the sake of satisfying her husband and bearing his children; hence, sexual submission was traditionally part of a woman's marital duty, a ritual that made it difficult for women to enjoy their own sexuality. In contrast, men were expected, and therefore encouraged by society, to enjoy sex.

This attitude perpetuates the myth that when a couple has sexual problems, or when one partner is sexually dissatisfied, it is most likely the woman's fault. This notion is still further enhanced by the taboo that prohibits a woman from challenging a man's competency as a lover. Victorian mythology presumes that men know a great deal more about sex and have had more sexual experience than women. It is surprising how many people of both sexes still think men are sexually more experienced than women, or should be, in spite of the obvious fact that it takes one member of each sex to have a heterosexual relationship.

The following case history illustrates various patterns of sexual inhibitions based on Victorian mythology:

Loraine grew up in a medium-sized city in the southern part of the United States. Sex was never discussed in her family, nor could she ever recall seeing either parent nude. She did remember, though, hearing various noises coming from her parent's bedroom when she was a young child. To Loraine, it sounded as if her mother was being hurt. While Loraine didn't understand what was happening, she knew it had something to do with sex, and she was convinced that it was something her father was doing to her mother for his pleasure and against her mother's will.

These fantasies were so traumatic that during her high school years she refused to date at all. It was not until her junior year in college that she met Harold and began dating. Harold was quiet and shy, and his lack of aggressiveness appealed to Loraine. They went together for two years and married the summer after she graduated. Loraine was still a virgin on their wedding night, while Harold's experience with sex had been limited to a few prostitutes.

Their wedding night was a tragic experience. Having no idea what to expect, Loraine was extremely apprehensive. Harold's attempts to reassure her were totally ineffective; he, too, was filled with anxiety (which he tried to hide) and was impotent. Their honeymoon was a tragic fiasco. When Harold was able to have an erection, he would ejaculate before he could enter her. His explanation to his bewildered bride was that he found her so attractive he couldn't control himself. Their marriage was finally consummated sexually a few weeks after their honeymoon.

Loraine was despondent at her lack of excitement or satisfaction while having sex with Harold. As she later told her therapists: "I didn't feel a thing. When we had intercourse, I felt absolutely nothing."

Harold kept telling Loraine that she should relax, that only her anxiety kept her from enjoying sex. He made it clear by his comments that he considered the problem to be her fault. His premature ejaculation continued through the first years of their marriage. More often than not, he would ejaculate before entering her and actual intercourse never lasted more than a minute. Loraine resigned herself to the conclusion that she was sexually inadequate.

Loraine was 30 when she took an adult education course in sex and marriage and began to ponder the possibility that perhaps Harold was at least contributing to her sexual difficulties. Shortly thereafter, she went back to school to do graduate work, and there she met Jim. They began having coffee with each other after class and became good friends. Loraine was quite unnerved when Jim suggested they sleep with each other: she was attracted to him in spite of her efforts to suppress her feelings and the guilt that accompanied them.

A month later they began their affair. Loraine was fully responsive and overjoyed to finally discover capabilities of her own sexuality. She was also extremely angry at Harold for convincing her that she had sexual problems. When Harold refused to seek help (which is still more taboo for men than for women) for his premature ejaculation, Loraine eventually divorced him and subsequently remarried.

## TOXIC MYTH #67
## Men and women experience sex
## in the same way.

It has been pointed out that our Victorian mythology perpetuates a double standard about sexual pleasure. The
Don Juan type of man is still looked upon by other men,
and frequently by women, with an air of tacit approval. A
woman playing a similar role is still condemned by many
persons of both sexes as "cheap" or "easy."

In contrast, the anti-Victorian myths rebelling against
this double standard go to the other extreme and insist
that sex is, or should be, the same for both sexes. There
will always be a difference in the sexual experience and
meaning of sex for men and women. The fact that a man
ejaculates into a woman and that a living human being
may, as a result, grow in her body for nine months makes
the sex act different for her compared to a man, for whom
the whole experience may last only a matter of minutes.
The anti-Victorian mythology would deny this obvious fact
of nature and would have us believe that, because of effective contraception or the availability of abortion, the
sex act itself is no more encumbering or emotionally involving for women than for men. These myths teach a
woman that she should be lighthearted and sexually free,
because there need be no more consequence for her than
for the man. Anti-Victorian myths teach her that, because
she need not fear pregnancy, she can separate her sexual
experience from the rest of her femaleness. Equal sexual
pleasure for men and women is not synonymous with
sameness.

## TOXIC MYTH #68
## Men enjoy sex more than women or
## vice-versa.

Attempts to determine "scientifically" whether maleness and male genitals produce greater pleasure than femaleness and female genitals are primarily an example of how our technology tends to dehumanize all of us. As in other myths promoting "battles between the sexes," it means that everyone loses in the long run.

Toxic myths, taboos and rituals about sex reflect our traditional attitude of having largely avoided this area of human behavior. Nowhere is our mythology more deeply rooted and more pervasive than in the area of human sexuality. If there is any area where individuality and personal freedom can realistically remain relatively free of social demands and restrictions, it would seem to be this private area of our lives. Yet it is not so.

**Our society's stubborn preoccupation
with sex and appropriate sexual behavior
continues to provide a social and
psychological climate in which toxic
myths, taboos and rituals, both old and
new, continue to flourish.**

This climate persists in spite of hundreds of available volumes about sex. Commercial advertising about new books on sex promises to reveal "heretofore unavailable secrets." That these books continue to become bestsellers means that the possibility of discovering such secrets still captures the imaginations of millions of adults, including those who are well-read on the subject and are veterans of varied sexual experience. This phenomenon indicates that sex itself is still taboo. The majority of adults may be intellectually enlightened and have extensive knowledge about sex and sexual behavior, but their personal sexual behavior and the frequency of their sexual "problems" indicates that obsolete attitudes and beliefs about appropriate sexual behavior remain very powerful.

**TOXIC MYTH #69**
**To be a good lover requires considerable**
**knowledge about sex and sex technique.**

The general emphasis on "know-how" in our culture seems to insist that a superabundance of know-how is all we need to solve any human problem. For many of us, in sex as in other areas of our lives, efficiency per se becomes the overwhelmingly dominant criterion of what is good and desirable. This toxic, ritualistic attitude teaches us that know-how is always desirable under all circumstances and that the quicker a person acquires sexual know-how, the better. This preoccupation with the importance of sex technique is encouraged by our basic training that we are capable of learning through our own experiences. Many of the attitudes we have been taught by the more pervasive myths about efficiency and success in everything we do play a prominent role in our love making.

**When two people are loving, caring and**
**open with each other, there is little they**
**need to know about sex that they**
**cannot discover for themselves.**

This natural approach may not be as efficient as reading a lot of books that describe all the techniques in detail (some couples even try to keep the book open while making love!); however, with few exceptions, loss of efficiency is more than offset by increased meaningfulness when we proclaim our sexuality to be a part of our lives too personal and intimate for us to allow the experts to tell us what to do, or how to do it. In most instances, a more realistic and more human antidote is to accept our right to enjoy the excitement of experimenting, making our own discoveries, and finding our own solutions to satisfying sexual relationships even if this comes more slowly and is less efficient.

Those who are aware of their deeper emotional needs know that sex is most gratifying when it is an expression of a loving relationship that has many levels beyond physical gratification. The acceptance of this concept is a most effective antidote. When two people feel open and spontaneous with each other and share the excitement of their discoveries of relating to each other sexually, the doors open to a deeper, more gratifying emotional relationship. In addition, they learn to trust themselves and discover their own ability to solve other problems in relating to each other without always frantically running to some "specialist."

We have discussed the fact that ours is a culture of experts. While expertise is often valuable, we poison ourselves if we rush headlong to an expert and have him or her tell us what to do each time we have a problem. Such an approach is toxic even though it may yield an acceptable solution because, in the long run, it makes us more and more helpless, more and more dependent on experts. We never discover how much we can learn, do and decide on our own.

## TOXIC MYTH #70
**Some ways of enjoying sex are
better than others.**

This myth reflects the ritualistic attitude of the new sex mythology about having orgasms and climaxes at the right time, in the right way and with the right frequency. The dos and don'ts of proper sexual conduct fill countless books with ritualistic procedures on how to make love. It is not surprising, then, that one of the most frequent complaints therapists hear from patients is that their sex life is too mechanical and lacks spontaneity.

Myths that teach us that a good sex life means knowing how to do it the "right way" reflect the achievement-oriented myths discussed previously. In this instance, the goal is to stimulate one's partner with the proper sequence of maneuvers. Success is then measured in results, the "achievement" of climax or orgasm. The toxic aspect of this ritualistic approach, even when it works, is lack of the deeper emotional and spiritual feelings of love. Lovemaking becomes a skill, an intellectual process of thinking, planning one's next move, remembering the proper sequence, rehearsing the timing, and so forth.

## More Is Better

**TOXIC MYTH #71**
**The more ways a person knows to**
**make love, the better.**

An advertisement about a new book offering a detailed explanation of 64 positions in which to have intercourse (or, for that matter, 164) is apt to fill the reader with intrigue and anxiety as well. Such books exemplify the mythological attitude that there are mysterious, or at least ultra-sophisticated, techniques and methods one needs to know to bring his or her sexuality to its peak. Victims of this myth believe that the more positions they learn, the more adequate lovers they will be. Not only that, but their increased versatility will be a gateway to newer and greater sexual "success."

### TOXIC MYTH #72
### A simultaneous orgasm is the
### essence of good sex.

This myth represents the pinnacle of success according to the performance rituals of lovemaking. It is exciting and important when he or she can boast that: "We both had orgasms at the same moment and felt completely satisfied." Such a statement places the achiever clearly in the winner's circle. The poisonous effect of this statement may be quite subtle: it fosters unnecessary anxiety that, on other occasions, they may have orgasms at different times, or one or both partners may not have an orgasm at all!

**It is taboo for a man or woman simply to enjoy sex without reaching an orgasm or climax.**

This is another "should" with which people frequently poison themselves. They swallow the performance myth about sex and how they are supposed to react. Thus, they deny their own self-validating experience that, climax or not, they simply enjoy making love and feel good about it.

### Was I Good?

Because the success-achievement myths have such enormous power, it is not surprising that sexual performance is a very important yardstick for those who are stuck in this kind of rat race. Rather than being centered on enjoying their own sexuality, many people of both sexes are much more preoccupied with achieving an impressive evaluation. For them, sex is a ritual in which their partner's evaluation of their sexual performance is of more concern than their own satisfaction or the lack of it.

## TOXIC MYTH #73
**A more experienced lover makes
a better sex partner.**

This myth ignores the fact that any normal person is naturally capable of making love well and fosters the attitude that lovemaking is largely a matter of skill and technique: the more on-the-job training a person has, the better qualified he or she becomes. Like a carpenter or plumber, a lover should have as much know-how as possible to do the job properly. Those who are caught up in this myth follow the ritual of striving to win the label of "good lover."

Once again, reality is the most effective antidote to our toxic mythology about sex: we don't need to be taught how to do what comes naturally. We do need to be aware when our well-intended efforts, often learned from equally well-meaning experts, actually interfere with doing what comes naturally in lovemaking.

Anxiety about our sexual equipment (Is my penis large enough?" "Are my breasts big enough?") is another offshoot of our toxic mythology about sex. Rarely is such anxiety justified, yet with millions of men and women this preoccupation persists, often to the point of becoming an obsession. This is a typical example of how many people disrupt their natural ability to perform and enjoy their sexuality by actually creating their own anxiety and making themselves feel self-conscious.

**Given freedom from guilt, a comfortable
place and plenty of time, we can all be
good lovers!**

Myths about the importance of experience and technique
ignore the reality that the depth of intimacy and, in general, the way two people are with each other, is the natural
and sufficient basis for satisfying sexual relationships. As a
result of the toxic myths about sex, the simple notion of
two people sharing themselves with each other without
anxiety or evaluation of their performance is all but absent
in the way millions of couples relate sexually.

## What Do You Like?

Couples develop their trust in each other by taking the risk
(i.e., tolerating their anxieties, fears or embarrassments) of
openly asking and telling each other what they like or
prefer, as well as what they don't like, sexually. This antidote calls for a willingness on the part of two persons to
be open and honest with each other in discovering for
themselves how to enhance their sexual compatibility and
heighten their mutual joy and excitement. It is a simple
and powerful antidote to any sexual difficulties that may
rise. Yet because of the many taboos and toxic myths discussed previously, the thought ·of attaining such open
living arrangements often causes anxiety and apprehen-
sion. Once the risk of being open is taken, these anxieties
almost invariably melt away. Usually a tremendous feeling
of relief follows when we discover that these tensions were
really our individual fantasy-fears.

**But you can only believe this for yourself
after you've taken the risk of being open.**

Incidently, openness can be verbal or nonverbal. The only requirement is that each person clearly gets the message the other sends about what they want, don't want or what new ways of making love they would like to try.

Many believe the myth that having sex is, in itself, an intimate way of relating, if for no other reason than that two people are enjoying each other's bodies. In the same sense, an ongoing affair is considered to be positive proof of an intimate involvement. This myth confuses passion and sexual attraction with the deeper feelings of love and caring that characterize an intimate relationship. More realistically, the quality of a couple's sexual relationship is only one indication of their intimacy or the lack of it, rather than the basis for it. Satisfying sexual intimacy, particularly in relationships that last past the honeymoon period, is a reflection of an intimate relationship. When the overall relationship is intimate, sex is usually good. If and when the relationship begins to deteriorate, sexual intimacy also deteriorates as a consequence.

Toxic myths about the meaning of sexual intimacy or compatibility have this picture reversed. Not only is sex erroneously equated with an intimate relationship, but in addition, when the relationship gets into difficulty, a couple will often try to renew the sexual excitement between them in the belief that this in turn will rekindle a deeper involvement with each other. The exact opposite is closer to the truth: the deeper the intimate feelings between two people, the more likely they are to want to express these feelings sexually and in other ways. A couple's sexual relationship is more like an indicator that tells them whether their relationship is growing or deteriorating. In most one-to-one relationships that have some sustenance and duration, the deeper intimacy begins to erode first, and this is reflected in a lessening of the interest, experienced by one or both partners, in the sexual aspect of their relating.

**John:** It's been a long time since we made love. What's the matter, don't I appeal to you anymore?

**Mary:** Quite honestly, the only time I feel you even know I'm around is when you're horny. Most of the time you ignore me. We never go anyplace anymore. You seem to be satisfied with your beer and television and then you want to go to bed and make love after you haven't spoken to me all evening.

**John:** I know I've been neglecting you, but I feel that if we had sex more often, I'd feel warmer to you and want to pay more attention to you. I get resentful when you're not turned on.

**Mary:** That sounds like, if I give you sex, you're going to pay me off by giving me what I want. I don't like to make deals like that. They're phony anyhow. If you don't want to spend time with me, I guess I'll have to accept that, but I'm not going to buy your time by making love to you when I really don't feel you care about *me*.

**John:** You don't seem to understand that I get angry when you don't want sex and then I don't feel like talking to you. Maybe if you were warmer, I would feel like spending more time with you.

**Mary:** And you don't seem to understand that I am angry at you when we don't have much of a relationship going in any other part of our lives. I don't tell myself to turn off. When you ignore me, it turns me off. I'm not being spiteful.

This dialogue illustrates how two people can see their problem from opposite points of view. John believes the myth that having sex is the way to keep their relationship going. In contrast, Mary is aware that her desire for sex with John increases with feelings of warmth and caring between them and diminishes when these feelings are lacking.

If you have asked yourself, "Is this really what I want to do with my sex life?" and have found it difficult to answer, direct your efforts and thoughts toward the concept of naturalness. Free yourself from the toxic effects of the myths that predetermine your thoughts and actions about sex. When we let go of these poisonous attitudes we can approach sex in a natural manner, free from the restrictions of all the myths, rituals and taboos.

# Nourishing and Toxic Societies

In our culture there is a junkyard of obsolete attitudes and behavior patterns each new generation is expected to adopt indiscriminately. We accept this inheritance of toxic myths, taboos and rituals without question. Seldom are they offered as options that we may accept or reject without fear of the consequences. Rather, we are indoctrinated with them initially by our parents and later through other sources of authority. Even as adults, most of us continue to allow others to cajole or threaten us into believing — or acting as if we believe — that this legacy is not only essential but also meaningful and enriching to our lives. If we are to avoid poisoning ourselves, we need to ask which myths, taboos, and rituals we want to assimilate and inculcate in our children and which ones we honestly don't accept and would like to discard or ignore.

During the vulnerable years of childhood, we are taught to comply with attitudes and behaviors we are incapable of critically evaluating for ourselves. We are taught that, to be socially acceptable, we must meet all kinds of expectations. Within most of us are feelings, usually hidden, that we have somehow failed. We assume that those who appear to have assimilated these myths, taboos and rituals

171

indiscriminately are happier or better persons or experience less pain than we do. We are taught, for example, that wealth provides emotional well-being because it frees us from economic worries and affords us the luxuries and opportunities money can indeed buy. Or we are taught that fame, popularity and social status are synonymous with a meaningful life. We assume that there are "successful" people who have it made and whose existences have Utopian quality the rest of us can only hope for or dream about.

When we believe these fantasies, we are the victims and become the perpetuators of toxic myths. We thereby poison ourselves (as well as those we love) with an atmosphere of tension and frustration that needlessly fills us with anxiety and feelings of inadequacy. We may live out our lives envying others whose existences are no more, or even less, meaningful or exciting than our own.

Myths and fairytales are swallowed whole (accepted without question) by young children. While we eventually discover that there is no Santa Claus, we often cling permanently to far more toxic myths without ever questioning their validity. Even in adulthood we may feel that challenging these deeply ingrained attitudes and beliefs is too anxiety-producing or threatening.

Presumably these attitudes and beliefs were originally invented and enforced as a response to the needs of the group. As the group evolved, some of these attitudes and beliefs continued to enhance its welfare and that of its members. Others, which may have been nourishing, became not only obsolete, but destructive to the individual and the group. Much of our "taken-for-granted" mythology persists in spite of its antipathy to the changing needs of the individual and society. In short, we live in a social environment contaminated with the poisonous influences of a host of toxic myths, rituals and taboos.

**As adults we have the freedom within our
personal and private lives to review these
myths, taboos and rituals and let go of
those we find unnecessary, burdensome
or in other ways toxic.**

Frank grew up in an area of Manhattan where extreme poverty and extreme wealth coexist side by
side. Throughout his childhood he saw his parents
struggle endlessly to meet their basic needs and
those of their five children. Frank was the oldest
and remembered the endless series of financial cri-
ses. Each weekend his mother and father would sit
down at the dining room table with the bills and the
checkbook. There was never enough money in the
account. While his mother was pregnant and until
she could go back to work, the money situation
would become even more grave and they would go
deeper into debt to provide life's necessities.

His parents were very loving and dedicated to giving
their children the opportunities that they had never
had. This was painful for Frank to see as he watched
their endless frustration. Their hope never dimmed
and their courageous attitude persisted despite the
fact that things never got any better. At times it
would seem as if they would finally get out of debt
and have some of the things they always wanted.
Yet somehow, each time, a new crisis would develop
that inevitably ended with their borrowing money.
It is not surprising that Frank became resolute in his
belief that the foremost thing in life was to earn
money.

He was bright and ambitious and had a great deal of
ability. In high school his teachers encouraged him

to apply for a scholarship to go to college, but the frustration and deprivation he had experienced, combined with the love he felt from and toward his family, made him resolve to go to work as soon as he graduated. He insisted on doing so despite his parents' expressed desire that he go to college and their assurances that somehow they'd manage as they always had.

On many occasions Frank would walk to a nearby expensive restaurant and watch the people coming and going, fantasizing what their lives must be like. He would envy the big cars and the elegantly dressed people. To him they seemed to be constantly smiling and laughing as if the world were truly their oyster. His first job was as a busboy in one of these fine restaurants. He worked hard and diligently and during the next seven years moved from busboy to waiter to captain. He helped his family move to a larger apartment in a nicer neighborhood. The family had what they needed and more. Most of all, his parents were finally out of debt! Yet this did not satisfy his ambitions to be a financial success.

Frank had a plan. It became apparent to him that the chef was the person who made the restaurant a success. He persuaded the restaurant owner to allow him to work as a cook. Because of his ambition, ability and willingness to learn, the chief chef soon made Frank his assistant.

He became an excellent cook and took charge of the kitchen when the chef was on vacation or was ill. He was only 27 when one of the frequent customers of the restaurant, whom he had known for years, offered to back him in a restaurant in which he,

Frank, would be the chief chef. This seemed the opportunity he had been waiting for all his life. He was to earn a good salary and a percentage of the profits each year. The restaurant was a success and Frank really began to move up financially. Five years later, he opened his own restaurant. By all reasonable standards he was now a successful entrepeneur. He bought a home for his family where everyone had his own bedroom (another childhood dream come true!). He financed his brothers' and sister's college education and became successful in various other business enterprises. In no way did his success abate his ambition.

Throughout these years there were three different women he wanted to marry, but he rejected the idea because he feared marriage would interfere with his ambitious quest for success. At 40, Frank was a millionaire and finally did marry. Now he had it all: the elegant penthouse, two servants, a country home, travel, wealthy friends, social status—all the things he had wanted all his life. In spite of his success, he was totally perplexed over his constant and increasing feelings of restlessness and depression. He seemed agitated much of the time and could only relax after a couple of drinks.

He felt bored with all the luxuries and material things he had, but shared this inner pain with no one, not even his wife. He refused to accept that achieving his lifelong goal had not brought the happiness and contentment he had expected. Instead, he found himself preoccupied with new enterprises and a growing anxiety that he might lose the financial empire he had built. He seemed to have no time for his wife and children. When he was hospitalized with severe bleeding ulcers he was furious mainly because it interfered with his business activities: endlessly working, striving to meet people who had power, or might be of value to him in new business enterprises. He could relax only through the use of alcohol, but now he needed it in ever-increasing quantities.

Frank is a typical victim of the long-standing myth that material success brings contentment, meaningfulness and a joyful life. He has dedicated his life to the myth that this would bring these rewards. His disillusionment was too much for him to face. He had used up most of his life in this struggle and it had not brought him what he had expected.

Frank had become a victim of his own life-style. He couldn't see any alternate way of living or consider any alternate values. His life-style was his obsession.

Then he suffered a severe heart attack and was told he had to retire or he would be dead in a year. He fell into a deep depression. Only at this point was he willing to undergo psychotherapy. He quickly discovered how angry he was. He felt he had been duped. He projected his dilemma on society, accusing the culture of having sold him a bill of goods from his childhood.

Facing the emptiness of his own existence and the meaninglessness of all he had striven for was too much. Frank stopped therapy and went back to his business, taking on bigger projects than ever. Three years later he had a second heart attack and died on the way to the hospital. Frank was the victim of the success-achievement myth. He was a hero and, especially because of his meager beginning, his success story was written about many times. He *should* have been a happy man!

We know that many long-standing attitudes and beliefs about human behavior are obsolete. These obsolete attitudes and beliefs are toxic to us in that they thwart our search for our unique selves and our attempts to discover the reality of the world in which we live. In spite of our growing knowledge, we allow them to persist, subjecting ourselves unnecessarily to their destructive effects on our emotional well-being. A society can be no healthier than its individual members: poisoned by toxic myths, we are less able to contribute meaningfully to society. When we decide we've had enough, the antidote is available to each of us: We can stop complying with the myths, taboos and rituals our gut feelings tell us are toxic.

Letting go of toxic myths is a very personal matter. It concerns no one but ourselves. Furthermore, a myth that one person experiences as extremely toxic may be no more than a minor irritant to someone else. It's up to each one of us to determine our *own* attitudes, beliefs and values and to give ourselves the freedom (if we wait for someone else to give us this freedom, we'll probably wait forever!) to experiment, change our minds and do our own evolving throughout our lives.

A society is nourishing or toxic depending on how effective it is in meeting the needs of the group and its individual members and the means it utilizes to achieve this end. All societies include both nourishing and toxic attitudes to achieve, beliefs and behavior patterns. The more toxic a culture, the less flexible it is in adapting to changing reality and to the changing needs of its members. Clearly, the present rate of change is unparalleled. Such rapid change signals an increasing rate of obsolescence for many traditional attitudes, beliefs and behavior patterns.

Because toxic myths do not hold up under the light of critical examination, toxic societies can be recognized by the extent and the intensity of the fear, guilt and shame they inflict (or we fear will be inflicted) on those who challenge their myths, taboos and rituals. Some source of authority — and there are many — is essential to perpetuate toxic myths. These do not accept questioning or challenge, although they frequently give the impression that they do. In essence, the attitude of a toxic society is: "You will believe because what we tell you to believe is true. We know what you need better than you could ever hope to know for yourself."

Toxic societies advocate the priority of the group over the individuality and uniqueness of their members. They demand extensive ritualistic performance and/or achievement if the individual is to be deemed worthy and is to receive the full acceptance of the group. Toxic societies lack the internal, self-regulating processes necessary for their growth and survival. Their existence continues largely through the control and repression of anything new or different that is not in harmony with existing, preconceived ideas.

Dead societies of the past (as well as those not yet dead, but dying) largely became extinct through their own self-poisoning processes. Each such society was, or is, unable or unwilling to adapt to the reality of human social and psychological evolution in one or more vital areas of changing human needs. When a society remains rigid in the face of changing reality, it becomes increasingly toxic as its inappropriateness and ineffectiveness in responding to the needs of its members increase.

Society, like each individual, must continuously discover reality through its own experience and continuously seek creative solutions that are responsive to its changing needs. One of the most difficult aspects of this process is the letting go of obsolete attitudes, beliefs and values, for despite their poisonous effects, they provide the comfort and security of the familiar. Holding on to them allows us to avoid the fears that inevitably arise when we confront ourselves with our need to let go of the familiar and experiment with the unknown. While toxic cultures rigidly insist on perpetuating established myths, taboos and rituals, a nourishing culture has a quality of openness that encourages experimentation with change. Anything a nourishing society has created remains negotiable and subject to modification. Clinging to the familiar simply because it is familiar is one of the hallmarks of toxic societies.

A nourishing society is a source of strength to the individual, and in such a society the strength of the individual, in turn, provides the principal basis for the stability and cohesiveness of the group. The highest value of such a society is enhancing the self-esteem and promoting the growth of its individual members. From birth each person is inherently appreciated and does not have to prove his or her worth.

The more nourishing a society, the less it must resort to power to enforce its rules. Its members appreciate the need for these regulations and take personal responsibility for not violating them. They feel its laws are their laws, not something alien that has been forced on them. Individual members adhere to the rules, not because they fear punishment if they do not, but because they are unwilling to violate their personal standards of acceptable behavior. A nourishing society relies primarily on the integrity of its individual members, and their strength is its ultimate source of power. A toxic society, by contrast, regulates the behavior of its members largely by its power to demand conformity. Its survival depends on its ability to be an effective enforcer.

Many of the myths we inherit were once nourishing, but have gradually become obsolete. Nowhere is such obsolescence more toxic than when it pervades the area of our intimate, personal lives. A hallmark of a nourishing society is its recognition that:

**It is basic for the survival of our humanness that each of us has a certain amount of psychic space in which we feel we are the central determining force, an area of our existence in which we are our own bosses.**

Psychic space is basic to sustaining the feeling of emotional well-being and the personal sense of identity each of us needs. Toxic myths are a prime source of intrusion into this vital space. The more pervasive and powerful such myths become, and the more toxic the society that enforces them, the more we can expect to manifest symptoms of this toxic condition.

Toxic societies adhere to the concept that those needs, attitudes and beliefs that are not sanctioned as valuable and positive are to be frowned upon, disapproved of or even considered dangerous. This attitude inevitably inhibits individual awareness and expression. Our humanness can emerge only when our self-expression and our ongoing quest for creative adjustment allow us to recognize and express *all* of our needs attitudes and beliefs, even though group rules may prohibit our acting them out.

Toxic myths create the illusion that the quest for one's personal identity and sense of self means that an ongoing war between the individual and society is inevitable. In a nourishing society the differences in needs necessary to sustain the individual and the group in harmony with each other includes the recognition of the validity of both *and* an attitude of compromise.

## The belief that society and the individual are innately hostile is itself a toxic myth.

On all levels of need-fulfillment we are constantly making choices: to exercise or to read; to invest for financial security or to spend for consumer goodies, to conform or to rebel. Toxic societies rigidly insist on the values they perpetuate and implicitly deprecate other attitudes, beliefs and behavior patterns not in harmony with or contradictory to their own. When we are unaware of this unrealistic and unnecessary war, we may become locked into a lifelong struggle (of our own creation) as we seek a final answer to what is "good" and what is "evil." If a man prefers living in the country to living in the city, he doesn't have to build a case that city life is no damn good. Yet a toxic society teaches us to do so—to explain, to justify, to account for our preferences. In contrast, a nourishing society says to its members: "I exist for your welfare. I have many and varied qualities to offer you. Examine them for yourself and choose what fits you best as you move through life. You are part of me. I respect and encourage your right to reject or seek to change what you find unacceptable about me, and there will be no retribution against you when you speak out about whatever you don't like."

# How To Recognize
# A Toxic Myth

Awareness of our attitudes, beliefs and behavior is the basis for change and growth, as well as for all antidotes to toxic experiences. Awareness simply means constantly paying attention with all our senses in an ongoing way to how we experience our inner selves as we interact with the world around us. This is the basis for the most valid approach possible in deciding whether what we are doing is what we really want to do. Or whether we are shoulding ourselves to death with toxic myths or other unnecessary compliance with someone else's rules. (All shoulds are external rules, not manifestations of our real selves.)

When we are interested in becoming more aware of ourselves, we can make a commitment to listen with *all* our senses. These tell us how we experience our own existence. Ideally, this would be a moment-by-moment continuous process of awareness. In reality, this is not necessary as *what* we do to nourish and poison ourselves and *how* we do it always involves patterns within us which we constantly repeat. This offers an ample basis for an optimistic attitude toward life because it means that we continually have new chances to modify our attitudes, beliefs and behavior simply on the basis of deciding for ourselves: "Is this really what I want to do? Is this really how I want to behave? Do the attitudes and beliefs I have accepted for so long honestly belong to me, or have my feelings and convictions about some of these changed?" The answers to such questions are not complicated because they need be based solely on awareness of our own growing consciousness.

The principal, and necessary ingredient for recognizing toxic myths, taboos and rituals is an honest desire to pay attention to ourselves. This alone can provide us with the clues about those aspects of our lives where we live with toxic myths and other alien concepts. To do otherwise means continuing to allow ourselves to be victimized and avoiding facing up to who we really are and what we are really doing with our lives. Once recognized, the characteristics of toxic myths usually suggest a variety of possibilities, immediate and more distant, with which to counteract or neutralize their effect.

It requires real courage to confront ourselves with the pain and emptiness that always lurk just beneath our consciousness when we live the phony life toxic myths dictate to us. Often we are aware when we are not being real. Usually we experience this as tension, tightness or other body messages. ("I need a drink or tranquillizer!) The innumerable ways in which we learn to avoid ourselves is testimony to the genius of humankind. Awareness of *how we deceive ourselves* is a starting point in becoming more aware of who we really are, whether we are doing what we really want to do, or whether we are robot-like victims of toxic myths and the behavior they impose on us.

It has been emphasized that a myth is toxic when the individual experiences it as out of harmony with his or her inner flow of needs, attitudes, values and beliefs. A growing awareness, a more focused consciousness that a myth, taboo or ritual is experienced as toxic sets the stage for a wide range of possible antidotes to the poisonous effect that these would otherwise continue to have upon us.

## Shoulding

When we react on the basis of how we *should* think or feel about our ideas, attitudes or beliefs, we are still responding to someone else and, in that sense, we have not become our own person. Such "shoulding" tells us when we are perpetuating attitudes, beliefs or behavior patterns that are toxic to us. Shoulds are not intrinsically bad, nor are they necessarily always toxic. Many of them simply reflect cultural values and standards that are characteristic of our particular society and are part of the process of living as members of that society. Toxic shoulds are those that are realistically unnecessary and that our inner awareness tells us are not right for us, those that are in conflict with the kind of person we really want to be or how we really want to live our lives. When we behave according to shoulds, it is important that we be aware that our conduct is being dictated by external sources rather than by our own inner selves. It is also our right to choose to have someone else, or some external source of authority, tell us how we should live.

In evolving antidotes to toxic myths, taboos and rituals, the first clue is to be aware when we are responding to a should. Only then can we decide whether or not to continue to respond, and for what reasons. Those who have reached a degree of emotional and psychological maturity and have a relatively full awareness of their sense of identity simply do not need shoulds to govern their behavior, nor do they need to rebel against them. When we are essentially our own person, doing what we really want to do, our responsiveness and behavior are based on our own, internal, self-governing processes. Only when we have internalized and assimilated those attitudes and values of our society in which we truly believe can it be said that we are really our own person and that our ethical and moral behavior really emanates from within ourselves, not from the fact that we are afraid we will be punished if we violate the rules. Only when the basic way of living our lives stems from our inner self-governing impulses can we really be considered to be reliable and trustworthy human beings. Those persons who function largely on this level demonstrate the human potential that exists within all of us for a love of self and love of others. These are the persons who live according to the teachings of all the great religions. They are the individuals who provide the real strength and stability that nourish any society and who contribute to the betterment of the whole culture.

## Labeling

Finding a common enemy or scapegoat to rally against is an age-old way of unifying and controlling others. Each of the nations at war, whether the invader or the invaded, sees itself as righteous and its case as just, and its propaganda is devoted to making others agree. Each side is convinced that the other is evil or wrong. It is by this same process that toxic myths are reinforced. Those who accept them are honestly convinced they are right and will fight for them. They also strengthen the bonds of their common cause by denouncing those who they labeled enemies because they have different attitudes and beliefs and refuse to conform. Myths that label people and reflect the "I'm good and you're bad" attitude are probably the foremost way in which humankind poisons itself against its own species.

**The myth that other human beings are different from ourselves is perhaps the most fantastic and most toxic of all the myths ever invented. Its renunciation is, therefore, a most powerful antidote.**

When we recognize this myth for what it is, we see the psychological roots of much of the historical conflicts between nations. In reality, our "enemies" are the *same* as we. Their hostility toward us, like ours toward them, is largely a manifestation of their frustrations, anxieties and fears, which have, by the indoctrination of toxic myths and other lies, been focused on us as the cause of their problems. The antidote to toxic myths about "others" is to recognize that all of us, whether in our society or in that of our "enemies," are victims of the particular brand of toxic myths of our respective cultures. And we all come out the same way: with manufactured enemies.

Meanwhile, more realistic possibilities for creative resolutions to human problems, which do not demand a human antagonist for their fulfillment, are lost in this endless struggle. This same poisonous attitude also pervades our personal lives when we evaluate each other, as "friends" or "enemies," depending on the labels we apply to each subgroup within our society.

## Keeping the Game Going

To understand when we ourselves have become perpetuators of toxic myths, taboos and rituals, we can ask ourselves the following questions:

1. Do I feel threatened by discussing or questioning the validity of the myths, taboos and rituals in which I believe?

2. Am I aware of avoiding or rationalizing personal experiences that are consistent with those myths to which I continue to conform? Do I push away from awareness any of my own experiences that are not consistent with the myths in which I believe?
3. Do I feel threatened by those who are simply not interested in complying with my pattern of myths, taboos and rituals? Do I consider them my enemies for these reasons alone?
4. Do I believe *because* I believe everyone else believes?

Ideas, opinions, people telling us what to do, advocates of every conceivable position about every conceivable subject come looming in on us from all sides. The confusion that most of us experience is in part because each of these diverse views have some validity. Each makes some kind of sense. When they are expounded by a charismatic speaker, we become even more susceptible to them. When we get the notion that others are largely in accord with these ideas and beliefs, it makes us more vulnerable to swallowing them ourselves.

Millions of people get lost and confused by the deluge of facts, opinions and answers, all of which are backed by the persuasiveness of various external sources of authority and others who have the means to simply propagandize us by repeatedly drumming their message into us until some kind of brainwashing actually does occur, whether they are aware of it or not.

Sheeplike conformity has always been an appealing way to resolve conflict because it is the course of least resistance. It is less threatening to adhere with a closed mind and rigid attitude to what we have always known. Experimenting with different attitudes, beliefs and behavior may be more nourishing and meaningful, but it also means exposing ourselves to the fears and anxieties of the unknown.

At any point in our lives, when we are willing to take the risk, we can take stock of those attitudes, beliefs and values that are part of us, those we have freely accepted and do not adhere to out of guilt, shame or fear. This is the most sensible way to discover our own identity. Knowing who we are and living as we really choose to is only possible when it is based primarily on what we have assimilated and made part of ourselves. This is the same process by which we develop new dimensions and depth as we move through life.

Self-awareness is the basis for maintaining our way of being in the world. Being aware of who we are is the best antidote for toxic myths, taboos and rituals we have swallowed in the past and a here-and-now prophylaxis against new kinds of poison and new toxic myths with which we are always being confronted.

Growing awareness of ourselves will allow us to sample new experiences while remaining less susceptible to being sucked-in or carried away by the power and manipulations of others or the emotional impact of new kinds of group conformity. Such manipulations are often designed to diminish our ability to remain centered on that inner wisdom within each of us that will always remain the most reliable way of discovering who we really are and living our lives as we really choose. Those who move through life in accord with this inner wisdom find a unity in living that is astonishingly simple. Conversely, we can recognize that, when life seems complex and overwhelming, this is a clear message that we are losing touch with ourselves and need to return to the inner core of our own identity, which is always there when we choose to look for it.

Toxic myths that perpetuate the "more is better" attitude accelerate our pace of living unnaturally. The potentiality of any experience is lost when we imagine we need more. We drive ourselves to move on (ready or not) so as

to maintain our schedule of achievements. We gorge ourselves on experiences, seeking ever more intense external
stimulation. We become addicted to a need for a constant
flood of busy material; when this is not forthcoming, we
become bored, fearful or anxious.

Such a shallow existence seems sad enough, but shallow-
ness may be only the beginning. The quest for more and
more experiences can become an obsession, an illusion
that we need an enormous production of new and continuous stimulation to make life meaningful. We imagine we
need more and more, while what is really happening is that
our senses are becoming calloused by a stimulus overload.
Patience and discipline become increasingly more intolerable. We demand instant relief, instant meaningfulness,
instant expertise, even instant intimacy. As our frenzied
efforts fail and we become more desperate, we may also
attack the problem from the other end and anesthetize
ourselves against our pain and frustration with drugs, alcohol and tranquillizers. In so doing we anesthetize ourselves to life as well.

This rat race life-style is testimony to the toxic myth that
we not only need to have more and more in order to expand
our self, but that these are external things which we must
seek in the world around us if our lives are to be more
meaningful. Thus, life becomes more and more complicated, and complication is synonymous with toxic living.

The recycling concept offers an antidote to those myths
that encourage us to complicate our lives. We can glean
endless riches from what already exists within us, in our
present environment. We can simplify our existence and
experience infinitely more through our growing consciousness and awareness. This is all that is needed to enjoy an
endlessly enriching process of living, which needs nothing
more than is already available—if we would only look!
Using our existing potentials to discover the excitement

and meaning in what already exists and is available to us frees us from the trap of endlessly searching for the more and more "out there."

## Uncluttering

Toxic myths can poison us only so long as we allow them to dictate our beliefs and behavior on the basis of the shoulds and should nots we learned in childhood and continue to conform to as if we are hypnotized. Most such myths are powerful only because people are honestly convinced that everyone really thinks, feels and reacts according to their demands and taboos. The pressure to comply is based on this fantasy that we will find ourselves alone and abandoned if we renounce what seems to be universally accepted.

Allowing oneself to step beyond this prison and into a temporary void of emotional and behavioral openness (experimenting with letting go of our conditional responses) sets the stage for new awareness and the emergence of new creative patterns of action that we may discover are more valid and harmonious with what we need and who we really are. We still can have the love and acceptance we want from others. If anything, this acceptance is more available now because we ourselves are more real, open and honest and have become more nourishing and open for others to relate to.

We can best discover for ourselves whether a certain attitude or belief is really our own or is largely our automatic compliance to a toxic myth by listening to the messages of our gut level reactions, as well as to our intellect. Gut level reactions refer, in particular, to feelings within our chest and stomach that in essence say a "yes" or "no" to whatever we are thinking, feeling or doing at the moment. The body does not lie and all kinds of body reactions will tell us what really fits us at any moment.

A cocktail party is an excellent example of superficially conforming to social rituals while, for many of the guests, their bodies are sending clear messages of how they are really experiencing what is happening. Casual observation will reveal the frozen smiles, persons who keep looking around for someone interesting to talk to while nodding absently to another person who is talking to them, or those who constantly hold a cigarette or a drink in their hands and listen passively to others so they will not appear lonely or isolated.

Toxic myths would have us believe that our emotions are the least trustworthy part of us. In reality the opposite is far closer to the truth. Paying attention to the language of our bodies offers a natural antidote to toxic compliance. When we are willing to risk listening to our emotions as well as our intellect, we open the gates to a more simplified (nourishing) life and rid ourselves of the accumulated clutter of countless obsolete or unnecessary rituals and taboos we otherwise hold on to for no other reason than habit or fear. Possibly our friends will still like us even if we are the first to leave the party!

## Conclusion

Whether we know it or not, each of us decides which is of primary importance, the approval of others or the discovery of our own unique individuality. The more we choose to move in one direction, the more we risk losing the gratification of the other. The more time and energy we commit to seeking the approval of others by rigidly conforming to the rituals and taboos toxic myths demand, the less we are free to satisfy our individual needs. Basically, the choice is between turning outward and seeking security and stability by conforming to what we are taught is most acceptable (and changing this as the majority changes), or turning inward and giving up this security and stability, and taking the risk of seeking a more meaningful and creative life by discovering how to stand on our own two feet.

# Antidotes to Toxic Myths

How we relate to society, how we go about obtaining emotional nourishment from it while at the same time avoiding its toxic aspects, is part of a continuing process for each person in whatever social climate he or she happens to live. Within the American society there are numerous subcultures whose attitudes, values and beliefs are expressed in quite diverse life-styles. These groups survive and flourish despite the prevalence of toxic myths, taboos and rituals that would be their undoing.

We can easily get so caught up in our fantasy-fears about social rejection and isolation that we submit to all kinds of social conformity, no matter how poisonous it feels. We forget that there are others, often a majority, who think and feel as we do and are also searching, questioning and experimenting with letting go of obsolete attitudes and behavior patterns they too no longer find meaningful.

Whatever the toxic myths and other social pressures each of us may have unwillingly yielded to in the past, there are always new possibilities for change that emerge as our self grows. New options and choices continue to exist throughout our lives; we are constantly deciding whether we are aware of it or not, to perpetuate past patterns or to let go of those we experience as unnecessary and/or toxic.

We can endlessly attack society's shortcomings while continuing to avoid initiating changes in our own attitudes and behavior patterns that might suit us better. We can use up our lives complaining about the failings of society: "I can't be happy because society is so fouled up!" These are nothing but convenient blaming games that only serve as excuses to avoid taking the responsibility for doing the best we can.

As our society becomes more complex, its regulations and prohibitions seem to become increasingly and often unnecessarily meddlesome. The heterogeneous nature of our society enhances this interference enormously. There is scarcely a thought, feeling or act that some source of authority does not seek to regulate. We have only ourselves to blame when we allow ourselves to be victimized by this social meddling into our privacy and the curbing of our personal freedom. We give away our power by the very act of responding to these external demands whether we respond by complying, attacking or defending ourselves because any response only encourages more toxic intrusions. In our private lives the arbitrary demand of most external authorities and social pressures can be ignored. We can turn instead to our inner self-regulating processes and trust ourselves that we will not become barbarians when we ignore toxic myths, taboos and rituals. This antidote process begins with our being aware that, when we unwillingly comply with the prevalent taboos and rituals, we are surrendering part of our freedom and individuality. Myths, taboos and rituals are toxic when we experience their effect on us as destructive to our well-being and to the meaningfulness of our living. They are not "objectively bad." Those who prefer to comply with some of the myths, taboos and rituals discussed in this book and find them nourishing to their personal well-being would actually be poisoning themselves by giving up something that, for them, is meaningful.

To arbitrarily label myths toxic or attempt to impose the abandonment of various myths, taboos and rituals on other people is just as toxic as seeking to impose their perpetuation on others.

**A major antidote for toxic myths involves recognizing that it is in the area of our personal, private lives that the acceptance or rejection of the attitudes and behavior patterns these myths advocate is most realistic.**

In our personal life our conflicts and frustrations are largely an inner struggle with ourselves. Usually we do not want to see the struggle in this way. It is easier to project the problem and imagine all kinds of antagonists and opponents (other people, institutions, political ideologies, etc.) we can struggle against. This is simply another way we can lose ourselves as we avoid facing up to the fact that our real work is within ourselves, and it is here that we can be most effective in living that way we really would like to.

It can be frightening and anxiety-producing to recognize the truth that we have far more power to determine our personal lives and evolve our own attitudes and beliefs than all of the external pressures that exist around us. Once we face up to this fact, it can provide a far more optimistic way of seeing ourselves and the world around us.

**Far more than most of us realize, we have the power within us to do what we really want to do.**

When we lose sight of this, we challenge the omnipresent external antagonists and "enemies," assuming they must be defeated before we can have our freedom. In these false battles the self is lost in the struggle with these "external forces" and we delude ourselves into believing that these obstacles to our freedom must be defeated. Whenever we fight others to free ourselves from the myths, taboos and rituals we consider toxic, we lose ourselves in the illusion that external forces are the cause of our frustrations and that we must look to them for the solution to our conflicts and discontentments. We ask them for permission to change and do our own growing. Similarly, when we seek antidotes to toxic myths by attacking existing social institutions or denouncing those who believe in these myths (i.e., fighting for this permission), we are again fighting the wrong war.

## The struggle against toxic myths is overwhelmingly a struggle within each individual.

Discovering antidotes to toxic myths means saying good-bye to those patterns we have been raised with and no longer wish to abide by even though others choose (or we imagine they choose) to continue to believe and comply. The struggle is not easy because toxic myths, taboos and rituals leave powerful imprints; otherwise, they could not have become so burdensome in the first place. The primary struggle to discover effective antidotes is largely against our own fears, our own guilts, our own anxieties. Letting go of unwanted compliance with these myths, taboos and rituals almost invariably evokes the pain of guilt, fear and anxiety. Usually it is only *after* we take a stand and strive to let go that this pain subsides.

Our willingness to risk experimenting to discover our personal antidotes to toxic myths is usually strengthened as we become more aware of the tremendous amounts of energy we waste in avoiding these fears and feelings: "What will people think if I fail to meet their standards or violate their expectations?" Yet, to do otherwise is to allow the toxic myths, taboos and rituals to remain like a chronic disease that subtly and endlessly saps our aliveness.

Because antidotes to toxic myths are overwhelmingly an inward-oriented struggle to diminish their power over us, it must be emphasized that the struggle is most effective when we go about it quietly. (It's nobody else's business anyway!) Those who find nourishing resolutions do not proclaim their achievement from the hilltops. Just as the struggle to find an antidote is within one's self, so the resolution of the poisonous effect of toxic myths is also a quiet, inner process.

Myths, taboos and rituals are part of the process by which society preserves itself and its values and reflects the prevailing attitudes and beliefs instilled in us throughout childhood. It could not be any other way and still provide us with the necessary social stability. As we begin to question various prevailing cultural values and attitudes and the mythology that contributes to their perpetuation, there is a tendency to attack toxic myths as "evil." This approach is also toxic.

**A nourishing attitude toward seeking antidotes to toxic myths focuses on our willingness to take a stand for what we prefer.**

"Put-downs" are usually toxic whether on a personal or social level. Even when we succeed in destroying a toxic myth by this method, we sow the seeds for the future myths, taboos and rituals that are apt to become similarly toxic. The free and natural process of change, the freedom to experiment with the new and discard the obsolete, is invariably disrupted when we become judges and condemn what we don't agree with.

## Re-Owning Our Power

When in adulthood we believe the myth that someone else knows better what we need than we do ourselves, we hinder the natural process of discovering who we are. In this way we make the process of letting go of what has been part of us and has become obsolete more difficult. When we surrender our personal convictions, attitudes, values and beliefs and allow these to be dictated by the myths, taboos and rituals of the culture, we surrender part of ourselves. As adults it doesn't matter what we have been told we should find to be nourishing or toxic: "This is 'good' for you; that is 'bad' for you." The truth will now be found in our own experience. To avoid being victims of toxic myths, we need to stop acting like we are helpless, which is simply another myth people sincerely believe and have never tested for themselves. Doing so does not mean we need to declare war on our family, friends or society.

**Half the battle of discovering antidotes
to toxic myths is recognizing when we are
fighting imaginary enemies.**

There are, of course, external pressures all around us that demand conformity. We trap ourselves when we assume that we must overpower *them* to be free to live our own lives. Personal experience, reason and our own gut feelings are potent tools with which to make sense (or nonsense) of any myth. When we become aware of those who seek to create guilt, shame and fear within us for challenging their myths, taboos and rituals, we can begin to be more skeptical about their reasons for forcing their mythology upon us.

Who benefits from the perpetuation of a particular myth and the taboos and rituals that stem from it? This question directs our attention to the motivations of those individuals or groups within our culture who most staunchly (and usually in good faith) insist on certain taboos and rituals. Asking it helps us recognize those whose active efforts in support of various myths are their way of perpetuating their personal status and sustaining their personal power. A hallmark of special interest groups that perpetuate toxic myths is their renunciation of the right of others to challenge them and their unwillingness to allow those who disagree to choose freely not to comply without the threat of retribution. These special interest groups fear that giving such recognition to the rights of others will end *their* personal power trip.

Continuing to allow ourselves to be victimized by toxic myths means we have chosen to ignore our natural capabilities for discriminating between what is nourishing and what is toxic. We then settle for less satisfaction and meaning in our lives. In so doing we are violating the very essence of the laws of self-preservation. Instead of trusting our natural sense of ethics and morality, we remain victims of the burdensome demands coercing us into behaving according to someone else's idea of what is our duty and obligation. This is a process of alienation in which we cling to unnatural attitudes and behavior patterns. As these become increasingly dominant we are apt to lose our personal sense of identity and purpose in life.

**Toxic myths are destructive to both the individual and society.**

This continuous suppression ultimately leads to explosive reactions that are extremely destructive to society. War is often a direct expression of this accumulated pressure. In more subtle forms a society can simply degenerate from the effects of its own poison as its alienated citizens become increasingly apathetic or passively compliant and give only lip service to the existing social structure.

## Don't Make Waves

From early childhood the numerous cues from the adult world about acceptable and unacceptable behavior gradually become so automatic that we short-circuit our ability to evaluate our own behavior critically: we just do it. As we mature, it becomes increasingly unrealistic to think we *must* allow these conditioned responses to continue to dictate our personal attitudes, beliefs and life-style.

Awareness of how we surrender our identity when we submit to this "herd conformity" is basic to discovering antidotes to toxic myths. The momentum of this conditioned response pattern is to continue to at least give lip service to the taboos and rituals we learned during childhood. Victims of toxic myths seldom check the validity of their fears, even with those with whom we are intimate. Often the truth is that *nobody believes, but everybody believes that everybody else believes.* Consequently, many people merely fake conformity. Nevertheless, they continue to burden their lives and waste their time and energy adhering to taboos and rituals they do not honestly accept. After all, we have also been taught that rebellious thoughts and resentments towards established myths, taboos and rituals are also taboo.

The fear of punishment for noncompliance with group conformity is itself a myth, for in reality there is no group mind. The notion of a group mind is part of the process by which we create our fantasies of expected conformity and social pressures to which we then imagine we must submit. We imagine we are alone and isolated against a united "them" who are all around us. Despite our fear of being different and therefore isolated, what each one of us thinks, feels and believes, is what many individuals in the same sociocultural environment also think, feel and believe.


## Thou Shalt Not Feel Insecure

Feelings of insecurity are taboo in our culture. Toxic myths teach us that a "mature" person no longer suffers from "neurotic" insecurity. The cliché "They lived happily ever after" is a trademark of myths that promise that one day our fears, anxieties and insecurities will end. They encourage us to believe and hope that we can find a way to assure ourselves that whatever we cherish will not be taken away if only we do what we have been told is best for us.

We use vast amounts of energy creating mythical insurance policies to guarantee ourselves against these fears and anxieties. We then pay the premium with blind conformity. Many people are obsessed with this endless (and futile) task of chasing after the fantasy of guaranteed happiness. Such a view grossly distorts reality, which is always changing. Toxic myths teach us the lie that we can reach a secure and happy state and guarantee its continuance despite the reality that the world around us is never constant, is always changing, and that we ourselves change inwardly throughout our lives. *There is no such thing as security, only opportunity.*

Similarly, we want to freeze (guarantee) our love relationships, too. In good faith, we promise each other something that is impossible to know: that what we feel at a moment we will feel forever. The happily-ever-after myth only serves to cheat us of the joy we can experience in the present, for any relationship, like the rest of reality, is a process of change involving countless influences and possibilities beyond the control of any human being.

## At This Moment I Cannot Be Any Different from the Way I Am

Recognizing the validity of contradictory feelings, attitudes or needs that we experience simultaneously ("My heart says yes, but my head says no") frees us from those myths that brand indecisiveness, conflict and confusion as "bad." The antidote process is expressed in the following statement, which validates all aspects of our inner selves: *I am aware that I have inconsistencies that reflect my varying, often contradictory, needs and feelings, and that's okay!* We need not capitulate to the consistency myth and thereby remain blind. Instead, we can choose to follow the unfolding flow of those attitudes and beliefs that do change us from within. This antidote provides the most reliable and stable way of coming to terms with change in ourselves and in society. It is an ongoing process that emerges from within. While there are no guarantees, this is the best we can do in seeking a creative adjustment and meaningfulness in our lives.

## Inner Feeling and Social Action Are Not the Same

Many myths discussed previously imply that the very existence of certain impulses or feelings threatens us with personal disaster. This notion creates immeasurable and unnecessary human suffering. It has been emphasized that toxic myths are deeply rooted in tradition, going back generations or even centuries, and are preserved by some kind of authority dedicated to warding off any threat to their continued dominance of our belief system. Such threats come from new ideas, new values and new attitudes that contradict the old. It is essential for those who choose to work against toxic myths, taboos and rituals and to bring about change on the social level to realize the kind of power struggle that is involved in making such undertakings.

However, as individuals trying to free ourselves from the effects of toxic myths in our personal lives, no battle is necessary when we realize that we do not have to openly oppose existing social patterns to live the way we really want to. Instead, we follow our inner feeling in seeking antidotes to those toxic myths we personally find burdensome and quietly go about the business of living according to our own attitudes and beliefs. In contrast, when as individuals we work to create social change and fight against what we consider to be false or toxic in society, the struggle is on a different level and outside the scope of this book.

In our personal lives the antagonists and judges we imagined had such power over us can now be seen as an illusion we ourselves created and have been perpetuating. Imagining that others are our antagonists because they disapprove of what we do is simply one way we victimize ourselves with the myth that we must have the approval of others. When we create an antagonist, rival or competitor, it is we ourselves who give that person power that we then imagine we must struggle against. In this way we cease to be centered on ourselves and our own needs and goals and imagine instead that we are winning one war after another, or recuperating from those in which we imagine we have been defeated. Letting go of this illusion means that the energy we would otherwise invest in fighting these mythical opponents can now be directed toward our own growth and evolvement.

It always takes two to play toxic games, one who perpetuates the toxic myth and imposes it on others and one who allows himself or herself to be victimized by it. In this way we get sucked into their game and lose our own identity. There may be others who see us as a rival and try to outdo us in all kinds of ways. Almost invariably it is toxic for us to respond to these people by countering their anger with our own. If we are aware that someone is trying to outdo us, it is only an ego trip when we decide we *must* respond and declare others to be opponents because they have challenged us. It isn't even a matter of letting the other person win, for that attitude also implies that we are in some competition. Rather we see what he or she is doing, what their games are all about and in response we simply stand out of the way.

## You Really Don't Need a Leader

It is a common attitude for people in our society to feel disappointed in their leadership. The myth that keeps us stuck and prevents us from finding antidotes to their oppressive attempts against us is the myth that we need to be led at all—or told what to do. For those of us who wish to learn how to stand on our own feet and learn how to nourish ourselves and have nourishing relationships, the idea we need someone to tell us what to do, how to behave, what is right and wrong, etc. is in itself a false myth.

## Tuning in on Ourselves

Letting go of the competition-success-achievement constellation of toxic myths means experimenting with new directions, developing new attitudes and adding new dimensions to the ways we see ourselves and how we relate to the external world. These new attitudes already exist within us but we fail to pay attention to them, least of all appreciate them. When we are lost in the rat-race of endlessly performing and struggling for greater achievement we remain "tuned out" to the many levels of awareness or consciousness that exist within each of us.

Tuning in means focusing on ourselves and paying greater attention to our own inner experiences. On the most obvious level of awareness we can then become more conscious of the meaningfulness, or lack of it, in how we use our time and energy. When we tune in to ourselves in this way, the meaning of living stems from centering our existence inside ourselves rather than on what the world around us says about what we are doing.

By generating our own excitement as we discover our inner center, we turn ourselves on. The turned-on person is highly motivated and centered in whatever he or she is doing. In this phase, we are then liberated from the toxic mythology with its demands that we live according to alien and unnatural taboos and rituals. Within the most intimate area of life, the turned-on person is more his or her own self than ever.

When we discover that we no longer need taboos and rituals to regulate (control) us and that compliance is a phony way of gaining the approval of others, we become more and more aware of the obsolete nature of toxic myths. Essentially we become disinterested and disinvolved with the demands of toxic myths one way or the other. We are not on any kind of crusade. We are not against them. We don't need to fight them. We are aware of their continued existence; but now we find that, because they can no longer evoke guilt, shame, fear or anxiety, they have simply become uninteresting.